A Sailor's Notebook

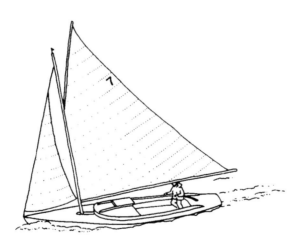

Richard Ulian

Drawings by Cathryn A. Wright

Earlier Edition Copyright © 1982 by Richard Ulian
under the title Sailing: An Informal Primer

Library of Congress Catalog Card Number 81-10381

ISBN 0-442-28665-1

Paperback edition published by Rich Publishing Company
P. O. Box 354, Cotuit, MA 02635, USA, ulyonsky@cape.com, 508-477-0403
1st Printing ....…...… October, 2001
9th Printing ……..…....….…… July, 2006

Hardcover edition published by Van Nostrand Reinhold Company
New York, N.Y. / Ontario, Canada / Victoria, Australia
Wokingham, Berkshire, England

e-Book design coordination and technical assistance by
The Dezign Shop, Falmouth, MA

Some sections of this book added since the earlier work appear in [brackets].
Text revisions, unbracketed, have been made.
Scans of original edition artwork by klhpublishing.com

15 14 13 12 11 10 9 8 7 6 5 4 3 2 1

Library of Congress Cataloging in Publication Data

Ulian, Richard.
    Sailing: an informal primer

    Includes index.
    1. Sailing.   I. Title.
GV811.U44   797.1'24   81-10381
ISBN 0-442-28665-1
ISBN 0-442-28789-5 (pbk.)   AACR2

For A. P. H.
sailor and friend

Deborah, Mark, Stephen and Pollena

And Robert 'Bud' Lifton

Contents

Cover: Wianno Senior Tirza *(7) on the famous downwind start leg, Edgartown regatta, 1973. Steve Ulian (age 9) on the tiller; Deborah (14) on the spinnaker sheet; Mark (12) on the rail with the spinnaker guy; Dick riding aft.*

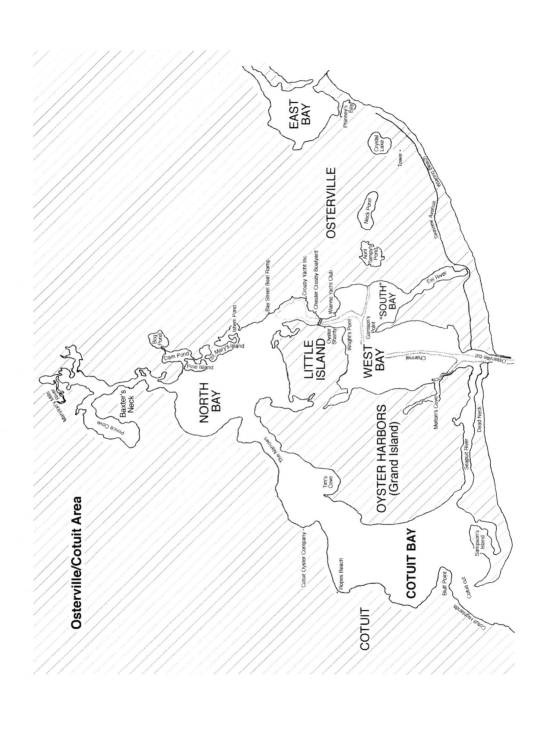

Osterville/Cotuit Area

EAST BAY

Phinney's Bay

Crystal Lake

Tower

OSTERVILLE

Neck Pond

Seaview Avenue

Wianno Beach

Aunt Tempy's Pond

Bay Street Boat Ramp

Crosby Yacht Inc.

Chester Crosby Boatyard

Wianno Yacht Club

Eel River

Bug Pond

Dam Pond

Isham Pond

St. Mary's Island

Pine Island

"SOUTH" BAY

LITTLE ISLAND

Oyster Shanty

Wright's Point

Garrison's Point

Baxter's Neck

NORTH BAY

WEST BAY

Prince Cove

Marston's Mills River

Osterville Cut

Channel

Dead Neck

The Narrows

Melton's Cove

Tim's Cove

OYSTER HARBORS
(Grand Island)

Seapuit River

COTUIT

Cotuit Oyster Company

Ropes Beach

COTUIT BAY

Sampson's Island

Bluff Point

Cotuit Cut

Cotuit Highlands

Waterborne

•

Why sail? Or row, paddle, or mess about in a small boat at all?

Because it brings peace. Contentment. Satisfaction.

It will get you outdoors. Where it is quiet. The air is fresh. Even salty.

And you will exercise. Use dormant muscles. Bend. Stretch. Pull. Balance.

And all this will happen while you float on the surface of a simply marvelous element: water.

A sailor regards Mr. Melville's watery world as the sinner gazing up at Father Mapple's pulpit – with a hopeful eye to the benevolence of an immense power, and a deep respect for its potential fury.

Water effortlessly supports huge yachts lying motionless

1

in the slips at dockside. But let just one outboard pass, creating a small wake, and each yacht gently dips and sways, so delicately does this magical substance balance these great masses. Stand on the dock and put your hand on a sixty-foot, forty-ton yacht. Gently push it. The house-sized object almost imperceptibly slides away until the dock lines take up. Such are the marvelous properties of water that one person can cause this bulk to move upon it.

Stand watch on the yacht club dock when the hurricane's edge sends short steep waves across a mere half-mile of open, shallow bay. The thirteen-foot Whaler outboards buck like wild horses, tugging at their painters tied to the floats. The floats themselves do a serpentine dance atop the chop and finally break apart at the butts. They swing at odd angles, the motorboats herding together, huddled, rubbing sides in the mayhem of marching white-frothed furrows.

Another time you'll find yourself in deeper water offshore, where the fetch is ten miles, fifteen, twenty. Let the fresh sou'wester blow and the waves rise up to meet and slap your boat heartily. Fingers of spray cross the deck, coating your face, trickling under your foul-weather gear. When the next big wave approaches, a whoop of delight and anticipation goes up from those riding the rail. But mysteriously, this one slides by noiselessly, on its way to another more distant rendezvous.

The water's surface has numerous guises – who can know them all? Off the southern tip of Ireland, near Fastnet Rock, compressed by 60-mile-an-hour winds into a shoaling Irish Sea, it rises into hulking waves that look thirty or forty feet high, depending on the angle of sight. Big and steep and threatening, the top six or eight feet of these waves – the breaking curl – can roll a fifty-foot boat completely over if taken on the beam. When the boat rights itself, pulled by the weight of its heavily ballasted lower hull sections, the deck may be washed clean of sailors, mast and equipment. One summer night in the late 1970s between midnight and dawn, seventy-seven sailboats racing to Fastnet are rolled 360 degrees. Fifteen men do not come back.

In the 1998 Sydney-Hobart race, a large fleet is caught by a sudden 75-mile-an-hour storm – not unusual in the Tasmanian Sea, but wreaking havoc nonetheless on well-equipped boats and experienced sailors. More than forty boats retire, damaged or abandoned. A major air-sea operation rescues fifty-five sailors. One man dies when swept off the deck by a thirty-to-forty-foot wave. Five others lose their lives. A rescue helicopter's altimeter records ninety-foot waves at the storm's peak. One sailor, chastened upon landing in Hobart after a record-setting crossing in a badly-buffeted seventy-foot ocean racer asks, Why do we do it?

Why indeed?

Reading the marble tablets in the Whaleman's Chapel dedicated to sailors lost at sea, Ishmael contemplates the question moodily. Then he cheers up and answers:

"In fact take my body who will, take it I say, it is not me. And therefore three cheers for Nantucket; and come a stove boat and stove body when they will, for stave my soul, Jove himself cannot."

Yet water also gives birth to life. Deep in its womb, life formed, grew, multiplied. The mysteries lying beneath its calm or stormy surface heighten the fascination of floating in one's own vessel atop this yielding but implacable substance.

You feel glad to be alive. You are captain of your own vessel – for as long as you can master the many moods of the sea.

·2·

Sailing is Simple

•

I first taught small-boat sailing when I was twelve years old, at a summer camp on the north shore of Cape Cod. One of the owners of that camp was not a sailor, though he was a fine athlete in his younger days, a college athletic director and an enthusiastic, successful camp leader. His name was, honorifically, Captain Delahanty. The camp had a nautical flavor, its chief pride being a fleet of eighteen sailboats.

Some of these boats were flat-bottomed skiffs about twelve feet long, skittish and frisky as puppies. In half a breeze, especially with a heavy person's weight slightly to leeward, they would go right over. We used to do it for fun.

One day a typically fresh Cape Cod southwest breeze was rippling the bay. We had just finished a race at our new sister camp about half a mile up the beach. I was asked to sail Captain Del back to camp in one of the skiffs. Our course was almost dead downwind.

I was scared of Del to begin with. He was jolly but ran a no-nonsense camp. He did not like accidents, especially boating accidents; the potential for damage to the camp was so high. I wanted to tell Robby Robinson, who ran the camp waterfront, that in this weighty breeze Del might be better placed in one of the sixteen-foot knockabouts. But Del quickly hopped into the boat and with a grin and a wave called "I'll see ya' there" to those still ashore. He was fully dressed, about fifty years old, around two hundred pounds, agile on land, rarely seen in a boat.

Off we went at a speed I could barely control. Del sat forward on a small seat astride the centerboard box. In the cramped, unfamiliar quarters it was awkward for him to move. Our speed increased as we got further off the beach. I could feel Del's grin freezing. The little skiff was yawing and oscillating. I was standing in the stern, tiller between my knees, shifting my own small weight side to side, wondering what to say and do when we tipped over.

At this moment I think I grasped something about the simplicity of teaching sailing: I said absolutely nothing. Del, an instinctive athlete and alert human, began to lean his weight with me this way and that, opposing the flighty tilts of the little skiff. We soon reached a point about a quarter mile offshore from our moorings.

Some of the larger, more stable knockabouts full of kids were happily jibing inshore of us, rapidly changing direction by sending the stern across the wind, to the accompaniment of some cheerful screams.

I knew if we jibed, Del and I would surely go over.

He turned to me with a question.

"Why don't we aim for the moorings, like the rest of them?"

He raised his arm to point, and the motion alone almost put us over. The wind had been freshening all the time. I bit my lip.

"Ready to – er – jibe," said I, casting a glance at Captain Delahanty.

"Ready," said he. But he had picked up my apprehension and maintained a tight grip on the thwart.

I saw my duty. Slowly I eased the skiff through the stages of broad reach and reach before I put the helm down. Come about is what we did, carefully turning into the wind so the boom would cross above Captain Del's head gently as we changed direction. Then we proceeded carefully on the new tack towards our mooring.

Although Del thanked me warmly for the sail I saw his puzzlement. He knew something was different about our method of changing tacks. But subsequently he seemed more relaxed about camp sailing activities. Not so often did the red No-Sailing flag fly when the wind blew hard. We were a little freer to venture beyond the buoys that marked the normal sailing boundaries. We could have more fun.

I learned that a new sailor needs confidence most of all. The way to instill this confidence is to do what will almost certainly succeed, at least at first. An instruction program will take many leaps forward that way. Or at least, few backward.

I do not know if Captain Del would have subscribed to

the above. I never saw him in a sailing boat again!

Summertimes on Cape Cod nowadays I give sailing lessons. I have taught sailing on and off for nearly fifty years and the more I teach, the simpler I think it is to learn how to sail. It can, however, be made to appear fairly complicated. Have you ever seen a diagram of the parts of the boat? Studied the rules of the road? Attended a classroom lecture on safe boating? Then you know what I mean.

Initially, you need to know nautical names for only about ten parts of the small sailboat. Several are familiar: *stern,* the back of the boat; *bow,* the front of the boat; *mast,* the rigid vertical support for the sail; and *rudder,* the blade in the water, controlled on board by the *tiller,* that steers the boat. Most people are also familiar with *port,* the left side of the boat, and *starboard,* the right side, but get confused over which is which. To keep track, remember that port and left both have four letters.

Rope is called *line.* The lines used to set a sail's angle to the wind – to *trim* a sail – are called *sheets.* Main sheet trims the mainsail; jib sheets trim the jib. What is the *jib?* That small sail forward of the mast.

One more and you are done. *Halyards* are lines used to haul sails up the mast.

That about covers the complete parts-of-the-boat course. It takes a minute or two to learn while we stand in the cockpit of the boat. The rest of the nomenclature comes naturally in the normal progression of sailing.

For instance, I ask a new student to take off the *stops* from the mainsail. He looks puzzled. What stops? Nobody mentioned stops. But a glance toward the ties wrapped around the furled sail explains what stops are. Soon the mainsail is hoisted and so is the jib. I ask one person to take the tiller. I go forward to cast off the mooring.

I generally walk the mooring back so we will sail off in a direction clear of other boats. After I drop it, I take my time returning to the cockpit. Meanwhile, the helmsman is sailing the boat quite independently of any obvious aid from teacher. This makes for a contented, eager student. I wait as long as possible before offering suggestions. I find reason to compliment a new sailor's steering ability – steering is not difficult. Sometimes I don't touch the tiller until we return to the mooring, switching it among students, and if the wind is favorable and the sailor apt, not even then. She moors the boat.

Going back to the dock in the Whaler is one happy group of sailors.

"It's really quite simple," an eight-year-old young lady said to me this summer as she merrily sailed us back to shore in her family's Laser after tip-it-over practice.

. Yes Gevry, it really is.

.3.

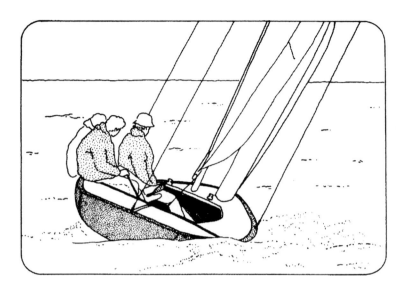

Beat, Reach, and Run

•

If sailing is so simple, what can be learned on the first sail? Basically, to steer and to have fun. To run free, reach, and beat. To make a couple of passes at the mooring if conditions are right.

To *run,* or *run free,* is to sail in a downwind direction. The wind comes from behind the boat. The sail is let out wide enough to catch it with maximum efficiency. Almost every student sailor can do this correctly right away. Next time out, however, most do not let the sails out far enough. One does have to keep alert to the direction of the wind flow. When it is directly from behind, set the sails out wide.

When the wind blows at a right angle to the boat's course – over the beam – the sail goes about halfway out. This is called *reaching,* a most comfortable point of sail. Almost all boats sail fastest reaching.

You want to make progress into the wind's direction – upwind. You can, though not directly into it. Trim the sails. Steer a course as close upwind as you can, keeping the sails full and the boat driving. This is close-hauled sailing, called *beating* when you go off a ways on one tack, then back on the other, making zigzag progress upwind.

Why give names to these attitudes of the boat's course relative to the wind? Because the names are a useful shorthand for things you will have to do if you are going to get from place to place in a sailboat.

On a day when the wind is from the north we cast off the mooring in the bay. The channel leads southward toward the cut into Nantucket Sound. We will have to run free down the channel. Fine, an easy ride. We let out the sail wide and go straight on out.

The shoreline runs roughly east-west. We decide to go west against an incoming tide. West we turn . . . and reach we must, since the north wind now comes over our beam. We trim the sail halfway and take off at maximum speed.

Coming home, we must reach back to the cut, the sail on the other side of the boat, tide's current with us. Then close-hauled, making short zigzags, port tack then starboard, each as close to the wind's direction as we can manage, we beat all the way up the channel to our mooring. Finally, we swing directly into the wind and coast to a stop at the mooring buoy.

Beat, reach, and run. If you have to get from here to there and back, you will normally do all three.

·4·

Preparing to Solo
·

Next time you sail, study the wind more closely. What direction is it coming from? Does it vary? Much? Constantly?

It does vary. More than a little. Hills around the bay will bend the wind. So will buildings, a grove of trees, other boats. Even if unobstructed over a large expanse of water, the wind will usually swing through at least five-degree oscillations. And the interval between shifts is normally short – not more than several minutes.

Some days major changes occur. The old wind dies and a new one ripples in. A 180° change can occur within moments, or the wind may "veer" (change in a clockwise direction) or "back" (counter-clockwise) twenty or thirty degrees.

Weather experts have provided excellent explanations for these shifts. The overall movement of high and low pressure systems plays a part in the larger changes. Patterns that develop within these systems contribute to local wind vagaries, as do topographically and thermally induced currents, updrafts, and downdrafts. We shall take a look at some of these patterns later.

But at the outset the important thing for a sailor to understand is that wind rarely blows from a steady point of the compass. The trick is to observe, be sensitive, remain alert to each change and shift. Better sailing will result.

Let's set off on our second sail. On the way out to the boat we mark the wind's direction. Moored boats generally swing to the wind, unless the wind is light and an opposing current stronger. Flags flying, smoke, telltales on mastheads will confirm your observation. In very light air, when all hangs motionless, wet your finger and hold it up. It will feel coolest on the side where a faint breeze strikes it, evaporating the moisture. Whatever your method, keep checking the wind direction every one or two minutes.

With your instructor you rig the sails, cast off clear of other boats, and sail down the channel. Beat, reach, and run for a while. You easily learn to tack – to change course in such a way that the bow crosses the point from which the wind is coming, filling the sails on the boat's other side. And to jibe – to change course by sending the stern across the wind's direction, again filling the sails on the boat's other side. You will see how to control the main sheet on a jibe, keeping loose-fingered so the line pays out smoothly without burning your hand. You will learn to duck during a jibe, to prevent the boom from striking your head.

Find an isolated buoy or a lobster pot and practice mooring. Easy does it. Approach so that when you swing directly upwind, the gliding boat stops just about at the buoy. A bit of practice is what it takes.

On our third lesson, you again first note the wind direction, then rig, cast off, beat, reach, run, tack, jibe and moor. You learn to steer backwards, by reversing the tiller when the boat moves backwards. And you will master the rudiments of anchoring, an operation similar to mooring except that, when the boat's forward motion stops, you lower the anchor and make sure it sets well and will not drag readily.

Next time out you may learn how to pick up a man overboard, much like picking up a mooring. You will tie four or five knots, all the knots you will need to know for pleasure sailing: half-hitch, clove hitch, bowline, square and reef. And you might want someone to show you how to whip rope ends to prevent unraveling. You sail, sail, sail. You now feel really comfortable and pleased with your progress.

Next lesson, if the wind is not heavy, you will solo. After half an hour of aimless but pleasurable sailing, you will be given a destination. Count on a beat and a run, maybe a reach. You do it easily, sail back, and land the boat on the launch or on a mooring buoy.

You can sail now. All you need is practice – alone.

·5·

Sailing Alone

•

I like sailing alone. Almost everyone does. Who would not feel the enjoyment and satisfaction it brings? Alone, in command, effortlessly floating across the water's friction-less buoyancy, propelled by the silent wind.

Because of its serenity, single-handed sailing often provides especially pleasant memories. I recall one particular day, beating down-channel and out into Nantucket Sound in *Tirza,* our Wianno Senior. The summer sou'wester had set in: fifteen to eighteen knots of smoky breeze, temperature in the eighties, whitecaps, and a two-foot chop, just enough to send cool spray over the bow. A perfect day. A day to sail.

About a half-mile offshore I ease the sheets and reach off for Bell Five, a buoy marking the edge of Horseshoe Shoal, well out past Collier's Ledge. No other boats are close. My own world, to do with as I please. I stand, sit, and wander about after tying the tiller so the boat will self-steer. I lie on my back in the cockpit, looking up at white sails and blue sky. Nothing was ever so white, nor so blue.

After a while I climb down into the cabin for some food or a soft drink or a tool with which to do some minor piece of maintenance. If the boat is steering herself well, I go up and lie belly-down on deck, watching the bow wave as it curls and froths. I take a full dousing and gasp when the chop hits just right, but the sudden dash of cold water is followed by the quick warmth of the sun.

Before I close Bell Five I cross paths with the Oak Bluffs ferry or another sailboat coming down the Sound toward Hyannis Port. I realize the time has come to head back, deflating for a moment. But then it is a glorious reach back to the stone jetties of the Osterville cut. I will be home in time for supper.

Coming up the channel it is a straight run, the boat lifting me in effortless flight like some great soaring bird. In the gold-touched ambience and light wind of late afternoon on West Bay I hear only the *whiish* and burble of water under the hull.

At the mooring I line up the Senior carefully before swinging into the wind. Heavy and strong, she will carry a long way in smooth water. While she glides I should have plenty of time to walk to the bow, flatten down on my stomach and pick up the mooring buoy.

When I finally have furled the sails, put the boat to bed

and returned in the Whaler to the dock, I dawdle, stopping to look back at the harbor one more time. I feel contented. The wind has died. In the soft light of evening sun white hulls glisten and glow; a gold-leafed cove stripe catches a last slanting ray and sends back a star-bright flash.

All is peaceful and well with the world.

6

The Smaller, the Better

•

How big a boat can one person handle alone? How small a boat can you have fun in? I believe a twenty-five-foot boat is about the maximum size that one sailor can handle pleasurably through all likely conditions. The United States Coast Guard defines a small boat as one under twenty-five feet, and a big boat, presumably, is one over that length. Our Wianno Senior is exactly twenty-five feet long, making her, I suppose, a big small boat – or a small big one. She keeps a singlehander busy enough.

On the other hand, much depends on rig, purpose, and experience. Alone, Joshua Slocum took *Spray* around the world.

She measured thirty-six feet. Sir Francis Chichester's second boat was twenty feet longer, and he circumnavigated solo with the benefit of some mid-20th-century technical advances unavailable to Slocum in the late 1800's. His boat seems huge for a solo ocean sailor until you think of *Vendredi*, the 113-foot three-master designed by Dick Carter in the 1970s for the single-handed transatlantic race. She was sailed across successfully, though the rig proved too exhausting for one man to handle and she did not win. I suppose one sailor could sail a boat even larger than *Vendredi* in open water. But anchoring, mooring, raising and lowering sails, docking – all the things we frequently do when sailing for pleasure – present fairly strenuous problems to the single-handed sailor in almost any boat over twenty-five feet, particularly in strong winds.

The beginner wants to find the smallest boat possible. Small boats are quick and sensitive to respond yet do the least damage when mishandled. They make ideal beginners' boats. If the boat is big enough to sit stably and semi-comfortably in, then it is big enough. For adults, this often turns out to be a boat of about twelve feet. Beetlecats, a popular class of about that length in my area, make good boats for adult beginners. An eight-foot Optimist pram works well for a small youngster who can tuck himself into it comfortably.

When learning to sail, nothing compares to sailing alone. Once you have had enough instruction to solo, you have had enough instruction for a while. You will not further learn to sail from a book nor from lectures and chalk talks. Certainly not from movies or slides. Nor by prolonging sailing with an instructor.

Alone, you have time to observe, experiment, err, correct. Each solitary moment teaches its lesson better than if accompanied by the instructor's now superfluous voice. Find the boat, choose the winds and place that comfortably match your experience, and go.

The hardest part often is finding a boat. A sailing school will sometimes let you rent one as part of its course. Your instructor may know of boats available. Sailing clubs and community associations in the larger cities are excellent sources not only of boats but basic instruction. Eventually you may have to – may want to – buy your own boat.

I would not recommend boardboats – the small sailboats that look like a surfboard rigged with a sail – for adults to learn or practice on initially. They lack inherent stability. The sailor provides the hull with stability in the form of his own weight . . . movable ballast. This can be tricky for a mature adult, though youngsters may pick it up a bit more easily.

Beachside concessionaires have been known to send beginners out in boardboats or small sailboats with a cheery "good luck" and not much else. Even if they do keep an eye on you, chances are good you will come back an unraveled, shaken-up beginner, confidence lost after an hour or two of wrestling – perhaps more in the water than on it – with a supposedly simple boardboat in a breeze. Do not try to sail boardboats – or any boats for that matter – in much over ten knots of wind until you have the experience to enjoy it.

Inexpensive, well-designed and sporty boardboats and small sailboats have shown a phenomenal growth rate. In the twenty years after 1960, 150,000 Sunfish were built for U. S. sailors. In 1979, 12,000 Windsurfers, 10,000 Sunfish and almost 4,000 Lasers were sold in the United States, ranking them first, second and fourth respectively among the fastest growing classes of boats. In third place was the Hobie 16, a catamaran.

Catamarans ranked fifth, sixth and seventh as well.

Surely Windsurfers and similar boardboats will continue to increase their sales totals greatly in the next few years. The Windglider was chosen as an Olympic class for 1984, the first boardboat to win this honor. Catamarans and trimarans are also winning not only popularity but respectability in the once proud and disdainful world of monohulls; witness the trimarans' complete domination of the 1980 OSTAR transatlantic single-handed race and subsequent ultra-high-speed ocean racing.

Many types of boats are available for learning and practicing. A boat that is well built and well designed will provide lots of fun and plenty of opportunity to learn. Find the smallest one in which you feel confident, can sit comfortably and feel at ease stepping aboard.

Then sail!

7

Getting from Here to There

•

Getting somewhere in a sailboat is not that hard. It may take more time than using engine power. It may not. It will normally take patience. Planning will help.

My point is, much difficulty can be attached to an essentially uncomplicated and pleasant process. If you can sail your boat safely and successfully in local waters you can sail it almost anywhere.

But do consider the *if.* I recall a man who did not. One summer morning I got a call from his wife. She and their twelve-year-old son had taken three lessons from me during the previous week. They were both bright, quick learners. She especially had impressed me because she could not swim, yet concentrated fully on what we were learning, never wavering in the very strong breezes of that week.

Her husband had just bought a new boat from a dealer in Arey's Pond. I knew the place because my own boat was stored at the boatyard there when I bought her. I needed four days to sail her home, a distance of about thirty miles, including two days sitting in Chatham harbor waiting for the fog to lift and a long-singlehanded sail around Monomoy Point over an Atlantic graveyard at Pollock Rip.

But her husband had never sailed nor been on a boat at all, except as crew with friends. He was an exceptionally intelligent, confident and aggressive businessman in his middle thirties. He bought the boat, a twenty-three-foot production cruiser with an auxiliary nine-horsepower outboard, and optimistically announced to his wife and son that they would now sail it to Osterville. He would be the skipper.

His wife called me after three days. They had safely gained Allen's Harbor, leaving about fifteen miles to go. But the sails had not even been up yet. They had powered down Pleasant Bay, skinned through behind Morris Island on a full high tide, saving the trip through Pollock Rip, and powered along near the beach to Harwich Port. After an unsuccessful attempt the next day to power against a fresh sou'wester, they had put back into Allen's Harbor. Would I please come down, help sail the boat back, and give them a lesson? She sounded a little concerned.

I looked out the window, knowing full well the tall pines' branches were tumbling and shaking – another twenty-knot day, the fourth or fifth in a row. I had returned the night before from a Marblehead-to-Plymouth delivery and lesson with a husband, wife and two young sons. I did not feel at all like doing it again, but still the next morning I found myself in their station wagon pulling into the Allen's Harbor parking lot.

Now here, patently, was a guy who should not – could not – sail his boat under such conditions. Sending his wife and son to me for a few lessons had not helped much. You really do have to know how to sail before you can sail from here to there.

We had a long, tough day despite the fact I had sailed the route often. It blew hard. Off Point Gammon, it blew harder and veered west, nearly on the nose for us. I took us all the way out past Bishop and Clerks ledge to get a better slant and to wait for a favoring tide. In that particular boat, sailing that far off Gammon against the stiff breeze and steep waves was like beating to Bermuda. They were a gutsy family and marvelously good-natured, but much of my energy went towards keeping panic out of the boat. The puffs laid the high-sided, tender hull over time after time. Nothing I did made the going easy. When we finally entered West Bay after five o'clock, I was as relieved as they were. The wife, writing a check for the ample amount I asked, added more. She felt they would not have gotten home without help.

I agreed. The man should never have tried it. His life, his wife, and his son were on the line. He would not have attempted to drive a car that distance without previous driving experience. Why would he try to sail it? Surely not to avoid the overland trucking charge . . . which he ended up paying to me in any case.

But once you do know how to sail, little should deter you from taking a trip. The longest voyage is done one mile at a time. If you can sail one mile well, you can sail the rest of them.

Not much extra equipment is needed for coastal cruising beyond a full-sized government chart, available at most marine supply stores. Study it for a couple of hours the evening before leaving, getting the hang of the depths, buoy markings and compass roses. Better not fool around with the miniaturized charts bound in book form. These can lead to reading mistakes under pressure. And each book includes lots of charts you will not need. You wind up paying more for a lesser amount of *useful* material.

Have aboard a compass that works. Even on a fairly clear day, from only a couple of miles offshore your own harbor will often be hard to pick out by eye alone.

Depth sounders, radio direction finders, other electronic navigation aids such as loran and global positioning systems – all are superfluous on short coastal trips in small boats. They will malfunction or distract, either way needlessly complicating your trip. A handheld VHF radio (ship-to-ship/ship-to-shore, monitored by the Coast Guard) or even better, a cell phone is never a bad idea but not essential for an inshore trip on a summer's day. Bring one along if you're going more than five miles offshore or off-season, when there aren't lots of other boats nearby to offer help if needed.

Stow good life jackets, one for each person. Boats with large leaks and small pumps can and do sink. Tow your dinghy if on a long trip. It serves both as a lifeboat and as a ferry to shore at your destination.

Plan to sail about three or four hours a day. Reserve time for a swim, shore exploration, lunch in a cove, cocktails, dinner. Sailing is fun and relaxing. But, like anything else, it becomes monotonous in overly large doses, especially for your companions, who may not feel charged with such exciting and satisfying responsibilities as the skipper. Give them time to have other kinds of fun.

24

This involves bringing decent food and drink or planning to stop where they are available. If I am skipper or crew, I do not use beer, liquor or drugs that alter mind or body until the day's sailing is done. It seems foolish to suppress judgment and agility while discharging a task for which they are needed. And why displace the natural high of sailing your boat with the buzz of a drug? Also, doing so may be illegal. More and more states are putting no-drinking-while-boating laws in force. Simply having illegal drugs aboard may result in the confiscation of your boat.

Check the weather. Not only the forecast (although it is interesting to compare with what later actually happens), but the weather itself. If you find it is too windy, calm, cloudy – too anything – postpone. You must feel comfortable with the conditions of the day or sailing is not very simple, nor will the trip be very safe.

Setting a destination that merely requires an easy reach can help make for a pleasant journey. With some luck you may have a reach again on returning. But this is so generally unpredictable a proposition that sometimes you will do just as well to pick a place you especially want to see, whatever the wind direction. If the wind is not favorable, plan at least to sail with a favoring tide.

The tide is predictable, and sometime during any given day it may be going your way. If your course cuts directly across a tidal current, sail near the slack, when the tide turns and there is almost no current, at flood or ebb. Your course will be shortened by as many miles as the average current-per-hour multiplied by the hours it takes to cross the distance. Though speed is not your object, you will avoid the frustration of sailing for twice as long a time (and twice as far over the bottom) as another boat making the same trip on a more favorable tide.

25

If available, study a tidal current chart for your area. You will find surprising ways to use the tide. Where it splits against a shore, you can time your coastwise passage to ride the last three hours of the outgoing current to the midpoint, then catch the next three hours of the incoming current continuing in the same direction. Such a split, a famous one, occurs off Newport, Rhode Island. The ocean is full of such oddities, and coastal sailors can enlist, rather than fight against, their effects.

In a small boat cruising the coast, fog seems to me an exaggerated menace. It looks worse than it is. You have got a compass. You know where you are and where you want to go. Your chart tells where any buoys you might sight are located, and the course to the next one is clear on the chart. Unless running tide carries the boat more or less distance than allowed for, the course you set should work. If the current does set you too far and you miss the next buoy, you are not lost. You know generally the direction of the land. Head for it, getting in close enough to make out a shape on shore. Take an educated guess whether to turn right or left for your harbor. Check water depths visually or by poking an oar or heaving a weight on a marked line. Proceed slowly. If totally stumped, anchor. Under normal conditions, fog is not accompanied by a storm. When greeted with patience and calm, it needn't bring great harm.

When thick fog and stormy winds combine and you are closing a lee shore, you do have to pay careful attention. Before the storm and scud roll in, mark where you are on the chart, the correct time, the compass course to refuge, and your speed over the bottom. If you have to come head-to-wind to douse sail and it takes some time – plot your off-course progress and fix a new compass heading. Average the yaws and swings of the boat to reflect the course you are making good. Judge or measure your speed continuously and average it out. If you were four miles offshore and are making four miles an hour directly toward the beach, it is wise to start listening hard for breakers before an hour has elapsed!

Provided your harbor is clearly marked and not ringed with shoals, bars, or rocks, you have a good chance of getting in without mishap. But if you are headed for hazards, you may be better advised to anchor or sail around until the fog lifts, even though doing so invites some discomfort and worry. The chief worry comes from the threat that really large vessels – ships – may cross your path if you are sailing in a shipping or ferryboat lane. The usual advice is to rig a radar reflector and/or blow a foghorn. Small comfort. Big ships and tugs with long unwieldy tows don't often pay attention to small radar blips, can't see many of them and don't change course for most. They can't hear your horn until it's too late. A collision is fatal. Get out of the shipping lane, close to shore or in shallow water where sizable ships can't navigate.

I have been caught in fog occasionally in a small boat. So have almost all the sailors I know. Not one has been hurt by it. Embarrassed, yes. Puzzled. Even temporarily lost. Maybe aground. But not hurt.

You will eventually emerge from the thickest fog bank, the harbor you have been seeking (or maybe another one) not too far distant.

And very likely – even though it was not all that difficult – you will feel proud of sailing safely from there to here.

·8·

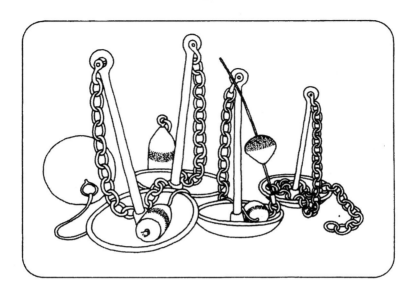

Anchoring and Docking

•

Watching another boat anchor or dock is always fun. The potential for foul-up is high; for danger, low. It is a second-guesser's paradise. Count on having in your audience everyone who is topside in the harbor fleet and half the people within line of sight ashore.

Sailboats do not have brakes. This is the source of much onlooker enjoyment and, I think, has more to do with a beginning sailor's uneasiness than any other factor, more even than the angle of heel (or tilt) the hull naturally assumes. A beginner quickly perceives that the boat easily moves forward.

But subconsciously he may feel the lack of a reliable means to stop. He remains silently apprehensive. Eventually the instructor suggests letting go of the helm. The boat docilely swings into the wind and glides to a stop. Relieved smile.

Coming up head-to-wind to stop at a selected spot is an art, which makes docking and anchoring touchy. The boat carries too far. Or not far enough. Then what? Go around and try again. Of course, if you had an engine, things would be easier. But engines quit and props foul. You really ought to be able to do it under sail.

When anchoring in an unfamiliar harbor, picking the right spot helps. Study the harbor chart. If still in doubt, rouse the harbormaster or some local people to talk to. You want enough water to float clear at low tide but not too much depth for the anchor to hold well without excessive scope. And you need swinging room.

When you see your spot, slow down. You can then judge the boat's carry more easily. If the breeze is strong, drop a sail. Taking the jib down subdues a flapping monster-to-be on the foredeck. The person handling the anchor gear will be able to work better.

Occasionally you will see someone with the guts to roar in under full sail, come up into the wind and smartly drop the anchor in a crowded harbor. Though dashing and pretty from the spectator's viewpoint, I wouldn't encourage you to try it with a large boat in a small harbor: anchoring becomes difficult because your boat may not have space to glide to a stop, and other boats are so close that maneuvering with sails up can be problematical.

So, slowed down, possibly with one sail dropped, you round up into the wind. Wait until the boat stops fully. If you slowly lower the anchor to the bottom, it most likely will arrive unsnarled. The boat now falls backward, pushed by the wind. The anchor line is paid out and then finally snubbed tight, so the flukes, the gripping blades on the anchor, bite against the drag. You observe for a moment to see that you are not pulling the anchor along the bottom. Let out line so the pull on the anchor is not angled too sharply upward. A scope of seven times the water depth is nice if the boat has room to swing. Often in a crowded harbor you'll have to do with less, but never under three or four times the depth. With less scope the anchor will probably pull out in a strong breeze.

Down comes the mainsail. Furl 'em up. Sit down in the cockpit and have a beer. You have arrived at one of sailing's best moments.

The anchor gremlins will find you early in your career. After a heavy nighttime squall you look out your harborside hotel window and see that the boat has dragged clear across to the other side of the harbor. Fortunately, as it drags into shallow water the scope ratio increases. The anchor is pulled more on the level and its flukes bite better. The boat may not go onto the beach unless the drop-off is extremely sharp. But a close escape will scare you and possibly mar the keel on a pebbly bottom.

If strong current has more influence than light wind, swing your boat up head-to-current, not head-to-wind. Before dropping anchor, unsheet your sails. Get them down quickly after dropping it or you will sail merrily around the anchor, creating a highly satisfactory mess – from the spectator's vantage.

In some harbors tidal currents run in different directions under adjacent boats. Edgartown on Martha's Vineyard is known for it. If the wind is relatively quiet the boats start a slow dance. They lie alongside one another head to toe, kissing, rubbing, wrapping anchor lines. Not much damage results and usually there are few recriminations, since the effect is largely unmanageable.

Using a two-anchor Bahamian moor (one ahead, one behind, then both lines led through the bow chocks, boat swinging as on a bridle) may be a cure worse than the disease. No one uses this system in Edgartown, where the bottom is slippery mud. With the crowding and the dragging at regatta time, if many boats put down two hooks, I suppose it might be December before everyone got unwrapped.

In fact, even in the Caribbean I do not remember ever seeing a Bahamian moor. Lots of sailors write of using it; perhaps I just was not in the right place at the right time. Once in the Tobago Cays we anchored in the gap between Petit Rameau and Petit Bateau, a small space with a strong tidal current. Our chartered seventy-two footer and a fifty-foot cutter were the only two boats overnighting. We both put out additional stern anchors. The current directly reverses. We had nosed in so far that when it turned eastward, our deep-draft boats might have swung onto a shoal at the east end. But the simple stern anchors held both boats steadily through the night. They were easy to get out in the morning, too.

Getting the hook out is usually easier than anchoring. But if you are planning to return at the end of the day, and you have a spare anchor to sail with, you can just tie a plastic bleach bottle to the anchor line as a buoy and leave it.

Go slowly when taking the anchor up. Think about it first. Perhaps the only problem not obvious is that the mud has to be washed and scraped off while the anchor, and probably the person washing it, hang over the bow. Harbor mud often has a strong clammy smell, besides being loose and runny. You do not want it on your boat.

If the anchor has sunk so deeply in the mud you are not able to pull it out by hand, try leading the line to a winch anywhere on the boat. Works well.

If your anchor line and someone else's are wrapped, apologize and unwrap them patiently. What gets tangled can normally be untangled. Next time you will anchor further away.

Did you ever watch an ocean liner or a freighter come to a dock? The slowness of her approach is agonizing. How little speed the tugs allow her. These huge ships also have no brakes, and water offers little friction for stopping. The ship has to be stopped almost completely long before arriving dockside.

The largest, heaviest vessel stops with greatest difficulty. But the same principle applies to the smaller boat. Its skipper must devise a method of arriving at the dock already stopped. If he does not, his landing will be accompanied by derogatory comments or – worse – dead silence from the inevitable audience, not to mention possible damage. It is an experience worth avoiding.

Proceed slowly, as in all anchoring and docking. Ease sheets before nearing the dock. You do not need the extra speed. This simplifies your calculations and lessens the problems if you overshoot. Try to land on a float's outer end rather than in the middle between other boats: if your speed is too great, you can slide off on the free side and go around again.

Have a person on the bow ready to fend off, protecting the boat and dock by cushioning the impact. Someone on the dock will usually do likewise. But if the approach speed gets really out of hand, have these people keep away from the space between dock and boat. Better to damage equipment than bodies.

One summer afternoon when I was thirteen my entire family went sailing out of Gloucester on a rented thirty-three-foot gaff sloop. I was skipper and sole sailor aboard. A boy from the boat docks who had accompanied us the preceding day had attested to my sailing ability so earnestly that the establishment's owner had given his permission for this arrangement. In view of my age, size and unlined face, he was reluctant. Rightly.

We had a nice sail to the outer harbor and back. My father, mother, older sister and grandmother were quite at ease. They did not seem to notice my mounting concern as we threaded through the inner harbor to the narrow end where the rental dock lay. The afternoon breeze was freshening and the huge gaff main was driving that lovely white hull at a pretty bubbly clip.

I was one nervous kid. Other boats lined the float, hanging off it at right angles in the breeze. There was only about seventy feet of open water to swing up and stop in. I sailed across in front of the dock several times, looking it over. We were going like a Cup defender. A boy on the dock – my friend of yesterday – wore an expression somehow combining grimace and prayerful hope. The owner stood behind, watching. My grandmother looked unperturbed, sitting on deck forward of the mast, knitting.

One space remained at the float, between two sailboats. I sailed into an open patch as far to leeward as possible. We were going much too fast. I did not think of easing the sheet – or perhaps I thought we were too close to the facing docks further to leeward and might rip the big main or scrape the long, overhanging boom. Perhaps. But when I put the helm down we had one hundred and fifty feet of momentum and only about thirty feet of open water ahead. In a blink the bow had nosed between the boats on either side, committing us to going straight ahead.

My young mentor stood steadfast on the float, frantically instructing me to try to brake the boat with the rudder. No use. I was too young, too inexperienced, too unfamiliar with boats of this size – and going too fast!

We ran right up over the float as far as the mast step. The low float easily submerged as it lifted our bow. Despite her new elevation – in fact looking quite pleased with it – my grandmother never stopped knitting. Everyone who had been standing on the float ran for safety except the boy, who made a brave futile effort to stop our momentum before jumping aside.

The owner glumly allowed that his boat would open up some and leak for the rest of the summer. And he had just had her caulked.

I did not sail a boat that large again for years. When I did, I made sure to approach a dock slowly. In tight approaches, I reduced sail, or eased sheets, and learned how to slow a boat with a sudden reverse action of the rudder.

Docking really is not so hard. Just do it in a boat you know and understand, in conditions you can handle. The same holds true for anchoring. Go slowly. Let the dock or the anchoring spot come to you, inch by inch. It will, and you will walk away with pride, dock and boat intact.

·9·

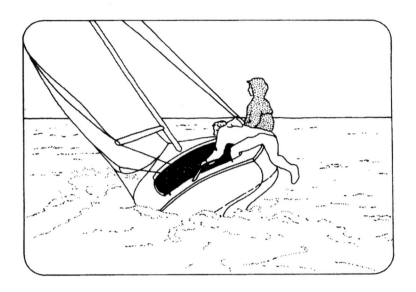

Too Much Wind

•

One day toward the end of summer after two weeks of cool, damp, northeast weather, the wind goes back into the southwest. And blows hard. The sun comes out and a light-diffusing haze surrounds everything. Smoke, we call it: a smoky sou'wester, the product of steamy, Gulf air blowing across the cooler waters of Nantucket Sound.

I take the moldy, mildewed clothing and shoes from the closet and place them on the porch to dry in the sun. This summer we live in a marvelously constructed, enclosed and converted water tower, the very paragon of water towers, in fact, sweeping in four pagoda-shaped stories to a porched, railed and roofed summit eighty feet high. It was redesigned some years ago by the young man of the property as his personal office, cottage and general summer quarters. It stands free, about a hundred yards from the main house and perhaps twenty-five yards from two other cottages on either side, the whole situated perhaps a hundred yards from the water's edge at Wianno. A desultory-looking three-car garage, full of the detritus of this enterprising young man's youth, lies close by. But the gray-shingled tower, borne aloft by the magnificent curved eight-by-eights of late-nineteenth-century Cape Cod carpentry, thrusts gracefully above it, above even the tallest of the neighboring pine trees.

No sailing lessons are scheduled today; my other work is caught up. We have lived here for only a few weeks, and I resolve to climb for the first time through the skylight to the tower's top to get a good look at the new weather that is upon us.

Even at the third level, I feel the tickling sensation that extreme height evokes in the back of my upper legs. I still have to climb a vertical ladder to the roof hatch, untie and raise it, and climb through if I am brave enough. I ascend until my head and shoulders poke through the hatch opening and, slitting my eyes against the windblown pigeon guano and dust particles from the long-undisturbed, widow-walked roof, peer at a most impressive view.

I look down over two quite different seas. The first, of swaying pines, is solid green for a mile in every direction except south. Not a house shows through the clustered pines, so thick and tall do they grow. A half mile away, I can see the only other Wianno tower like mine. Its top shows above a sea of pine-green with waves in pale and darker shades, like fields of long grass on a windy day.

The second sea, to the south, is Nantucket Sound, deep blue at its nearer reaches, white-blue far off where horizon meets water, the whole surface frothed with whitecaps. Only two sailboats are out this morning, no doubt because of the wind's strength. They have just left the safety of Osterville cut and from this distance – perhaps a mile – look like playthings politely nodding and bowing to each other in a toy-store window.

Lots of wind today. The wind is surely twenty-five knots, gusting higher. I watch the two boats for a while. One, then the other, turns and runs back for the cut. They are small boats. Better to sail in the inner bays – shallow West Bay, the narrow Seapuit River protected by its dune barrier, Cotuit Bay, through the Narrows into wide, safe North Bay and back under the drawbridge to a West Bay mooring. A pleasant sail, and today all a small-boat sailor can handle without strenuous athletics and some discomfort.

I suppose that is the secret of heavy-weather sailing in a small boat: not to undertake more than you, or it, can handle. Unlike the ocean racer or offshore cruiser, who may be days or weeks from landfall and must take whatever weather comes, the small-boat sailor can choose. It is not a luxury to brush aside.

The amount of wind you can handle in a certain boat depends on many things: your skills, the boat's inherent stability and condition, wave heights, the nature of the shoreline and bottom, the size of the body of water, the direction of the wind. Your own common sense and emotions will be the best guides. Common sense should keep you out of extreme conditions: gale winds, lightning storms. On borderline days, if you are standing on shore feeling frightened and you are not accompanied by someone more experienced and secure, do not go. You have a good chance of losing more than you will gain from the experience. But if you feel fairly confident, although challenged, and can successfully visualize the sequences necessary to rig, cast off, sail, and most importantly, moor the boat, go. You will learn from it, even if there are some goof-ups.

The practical limit is the durability of the boat's gear. When the wind reaches gear-buster velocity – different for differing boats and even for the same boat handled by different sailors – stay put. Many small boats will start to break masts, booms, tillers, and blow out sails in winds of twenty-five or thirty knots. The latter wind speed is technically a gale.

Sailors traditionally use the term *knot* to delineate wind speed or, more loosely, a nautical mile. Ten-knot winds travel about $11^1/_2$ miles per hour. The number is about 15 percent higher expressed in miles per hour, as a nautical mile is about 15 percent longer than a land mile. A knot strictly defined = one nautical mile per hour, a unit of speed. Reversing from land miles per hour to knots, a 23-mile-per-hour wind is blowing at 20 knots, about 13 percent lower numerically, as the reduction in length of a land mile from a nautical mile is about 13 percent.

Increasing the numerical value (from knots to miles per hour) use the 15-percent factor; decreasing, use 13 percent. If you can't remember which, use a compromise 14 percent factor to convert in either direction and you will not go far wrong. Miles-per-hour will always be the higher number when expressing the same speed.

At 40 knots (46 miles per hour) experts can sail well-set-up small boats without breaking equipment or bodies. Several times I have seen six or eight of this country's better Laser sailors race most of the day in 35 knots of wind in protected waters. On those same days, while on patrol in a Whaler, I have helped to tow in 20 or more broken-down Lasers and their waterlogged skippers – all good sailors, but not quite that good. Few are.

Lots of sailors are seriously frightened by trying to negotiate heavy weather prematurely. I do not advise taking beginners out in more than 15-knot winds in small boats. Many a day on our bay the southwester fills in too strongly while the kids, beginners or intermediate-level sailors, three or four to a boat, are out taking lessons. Sometimes the instructions to start for home come a little bit late. The boats come careening back to the dock, running free, some of the kids white-faced and white-knuckled, matching all too well the white-capped complexion of the bay. A few of the landings can only be described as "crash." No great physical harm is done, but the mental trauma hurts. The fear of being out of control, unable to steer, heeling too far, about to jibe, and heading straight for trouble is a fear that stays with a youngster too long. It is worth avoiding.

By the way, this is one time beginning sailors always seem to put their sails way out when running free. They feel that, since letting the sail out on a beat or reach slows the boat, it will do likewise on a run. It will not. What will slow the boat is to haul the sail in as far as possible, presenting less of its face to the wind. Sometimes this is hard to do, as a boat with a small rudder will want to round up when you trim in. Then you might just as well round up, drop the sails, and come in under a bare pole. The breeze pressing on the hull and rigging will move you downwind at a smart pace – sufficient for steering.

In general, avoid any conditions that frighten you. Be honest with yourself. When you can function in logical sequences of action, you and a good boat can handle almost anything you will encounter. But you must build up to it in gradual steps.

Any seasoned sailor can tell you his share of heavy weather stories. In fact he will be glad to. But do not plan to be involved in your own until you are ready and confident.

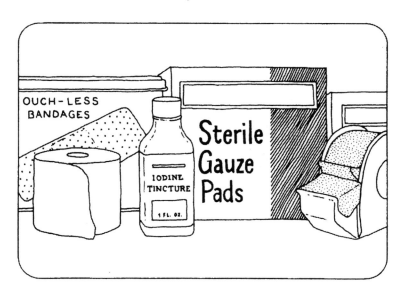

OUCH-LESS BANDAGES
IODINE TINCTURE
1 FL. OZ.
Sterile Gauze Pads

Danger in a Small Boat

·

In sixty-eight years of sailing I have yet to see an injury that needed more than a bandage to fix. I have seldom even *heard* of more serious accidents in an area where I have sailed. There are plenty of spills, chills, dunkings, difficulties; excitement is not lacking. But the injury level is low.

I am talking about recreational small-boat sailing in protected coastal waters and lakes. Offshore sailing or racing in any boat can create quite different circumstances.

A chief unlooked-for danger among those that do exist for small-boat sailors seems to lurk on land – or over land – in the form of overhead power lines strung across parking areas. The last direction a sailor might look for danger in a parking lot is up. But power lines have been responsible for the deaths of several young people in recent years. The metal masts now in general use all too frequently extend to the height of many wires, especially if the boat is already sitting up on a trailer or being lifted. If the mast touches a live wire, instant death can result: anyone touching the boat can become a conduit to the ground for whatever electric current is carried by the wire.

Some boat manufacturers now place warnings at the mast step or partners. Perhaps soon all will. Sailing instructors should drive home the point. Parking ramps and rigging and launching areas obviously ought to be cleared of these hazards. If you see one that is not, talk to the management. Meantime, exercise caution!

Poor judgment can put you in danger any time, of course. Particularly, use care in matching the sailing conditions of the day with your experience level, as I have said. Once that is done, little else threatens.

Lightning ought to be mentioned, though the chances of a strike on a boat are just as slim as on land. I have never seen a boat struck nor met anyone who claimed to, although I have read of such instances. Good sense would encourage one not to be near a tall object, the mast, surrounded by a level plain of water during an electrical storm. Get ashore if possible.

Most small sailboats now carry built-in flotation materials. The boats will fill with water but will not sink. Unballasted wooden boats without keels will usually float even when full of water. In the event of accident, so long as a boat floats, even nearly submerged, the best protection is to stay with it until rescued. In a heavily ballasted wooden boat or in a plastic or metal boat without flotation, life jackets are essential. For that matter, *every* boat should carry them, and the Coast Guard so requires. And people should not participate in water sports without being able to swim adequately, except perhaps under very controlled and guarded conditions.

Racing drastically increases the danger of collision. When the boats are much over sixteen feet long or are going fast, serious personal injuries can occur. On a race course with large yachts tacking close-hauled through a fleet of small boats, the chance exists of a small boat being blind-sided by a much larger yacht. The smaller boat will almost certainly be seriously damaged, its people thrown into the water. If you ever find yourself on a course like this, station one crew to leeward on lookout. Remonstrate with the race committee later.

In racing, a hidden danger, though rare, is a jibe by a boat close beside you. Her boom sweeps very low across your cockpit. Her crew is ready for a jibe. You and your crew may not be; in fact, you may have your backs turned to the danger. I have known people to be knocked out of their boats unconscious this way, with long-term injury resulting.

People do go overboard from small boats frequently, especially in races. Recovery is usually quick; it is no great trick to put a maneuverable small boat in position and make the pickup over its low freeboard. Sea and wind conditions are not usually extreme; long before a storm strikes full force, the small-boat sailor generally has picked up his mooring, snugged the boat down, and is watching the furies through a picture window.

Offshore yachts have a different problem. Far from safe harbor, they must slog through whatever the weather. A person overboard in extreme conditions poses a touchy problem and a severe test of skills, much written of in books about offshore sailing. Safety harnesses and strong, integral tracks to clip them onto, running the deck's length, are required in most offshore events. It is just too unrealistic to count on bringing exhausted crew back over the high-sided offshore boats, even if you can return and find them in time. It is a chancy task.

The small-boat sailor, sailing for recreation in relatively safe waters, might do well to remember some special circumstances that involve jeopardy for him. Single-handing is one. If a solo sailor falls overboard, especially when the boat is set up to self-steer, he has suddenly bought lots of trouble. Wearing a life jacket will help, but that still may leave a long swim home. Trail a long line over the stern in rough conditions and you will have something to grab onto.

Be extra careful when you are the only adult sailing with young children. The risk is not so much that they will fall overboard – you and they will both be guarding closely against that – but that you might. It would put the youngsters in a very tough situation.

One flat, calm Monday when my sons, Mark and Steve, were eight and five years old, they accompanied me after a weekend of racing. We set out to deliver the boat from Harwich Port to Hyannis Port, perhaps ten miles, preparatory to the following weekend's regatta. The sea was so calm off Harwich Port that we accepted an offered tow from friends who already had their own Senior and one other in tow. Within an hour the southwest breeze came on strongly, opposing the ebb tide. Near Point Gammon, off Hyannis, a steep four-foot sea developed. The Senior under tow ahead of us took some big waves over her bow that finally knocked the spinnaker pole loose. We were being thrown around in our boat too. I got the life jackets out of the cuddy and put them in the cockpit but not on the kids or myself.

The anchor was lashed on deck at the bow cleat. After raising it, I had left it there for use at Hyannis Port. I went forward to secure it better, rigging a part of the half-inch anchor line tautly from the bow cleat back around the mast. This used some of the extra line that had been lying around on deck and helped make a firmer tie-down for the anchor.

Before long it became too rough to continue towing all three boats. I put up the mainsail only. We were not quite around Gammon yet, but we cast off the tow and sailed for Hyannis Port.

The highest waves were now five or six feet, very sharp and steep. Several washed over our bow, loosening the anchor just enough to concern me. In hindsight, I should have left it. But I gave the tiller to Steve, already a fairly good helmsman. I asked Mark to keep an eye on me and went forward.

I was facing aft working on the anchor lashings when I heard Mark yell.

"Look out, Dad! It's a monster."

Before I could look the deck dropped away from my feet in a dizzying motion. I gripped the line that I had lashed between cleat and mast and held it tightly. I was thrown clear overboard to leeward. The nylon line I held stretched with the strain. Under the boat I went, looking up through solid green water. The wave passed, and I came to the surface, holding the line. Mark, with great presence of mind, was positioned right above me holding out a life jacket.

"Luff up. Luff up!" I shouted.

Steve came up into the wind, and the next wave floated me back aboard, helped by Mark's strong tugs.

We were all sobered by that incident. We discussed what

the boys would have done if I had been forced to accept the life jacket and swim for it. Could they have picked me up? Doubtful in those conditions, at their ages. Could I have made it to the Gammon shore? Probably, with the jacket – it was less than half a mile, and the breeze was blowing onshore, although the tide was moving laterally and slightly offshore quite swiftly. Could they have sailed in alone? Most likely, but they might have had to beach the boat if they could not round Point Gammon against a hard wind and steep waves.

Do not go forward, or to the extreme aft end of the boat either, in such conditions of weather and crew. If you must, wear your lifejacket, make sure a jackline (strong safety line installed on deck from bow to stern) is rigged and attach yourself via a good harness firmly to it.

One other danger may not be obvious to beginning sailors. It occurs when a small, easily capsized boat, perhaps a boardboat, is sailed in a strong offshore breeze. This applies as well to a light rowboat or canoe, especially on a large body of water.

When the wind blows off the land, even at twenty-five knots or more, the water near the beach is only slightly rippled, and flat and harmless-looking. The force of the breeze for several hundred yards outward is reduced by the shelter of houses, trees, and high ground. A beginner may be misled. He sails handily out to where the full weight of the breeze is suddenly felt. Then he finds it is too much. Worse, the route back to safety now lies directly upwind. It also opposes the direction of the waves, which have grown large with the increase in distance from shore.

This situation can create panic. Should a boardboat capsize it will be blown further offshore, very possibly at a faster rate of speed than a good swimmer can maintain in attempting to catch it. A rescue is required, and if no rescue boat responds quickly the potential for tragedy exists. When the wind blows offshore with strength, take extra care not to venture beyond your capabilities. If you are not yet expert and have no rescue boat standing by, do not sail a boardboat in strong offshore breezes. Or row, canoe or kayak.

Small-boat sailing does have its dangers. Although they are few and infrequently result in accident, the penalties can be so great that careful thought and good judgment are required before setting out to sail.

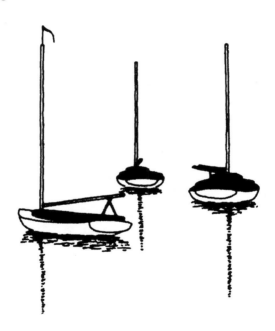

·11·

A Sail to the Vineyard

·

The August day dawns sunny and warm. A southwest breeze has filled in, swaying pine branches in an increasing cadence.

From the windows of my converted water tower I watch the motion of the pine trees. By gauging the extent of the branches' sway, one can judge pretty well the weight of the wind and the state of Nantucket Sound.

Today I especially want to know these things. I plan to sail to Martha's Vineyard, about fifteen miles across the sound to Edgartown or perhaps ten to Oak Bluffs. I will sail wherever wind and tide allow.

At the club dock on West Bay the harbor chop is beginning to show white caps. The windspeed indicator paddle on the clubhouse roof blurs as it spins – I would guess about eighteen knots without going inside to read the dial. The Whaler's old Johnson 40-horse engine starts on the second try; good thing I changed the plugs again yesterday. After a short ride out to the mooring, sliding slowly past rows of Beetles, larger plastic auxiliaries, other Seniors and several traditional wooden cruising boats in the outer tier, I reach a cluster of four Wianno Seniors lying snugly near the far shore. Ours – white topsides, bright-finished oak, mahogany and teak trim, tan deck – is the last one in the line. As always when I pull the Whaler in behind the transom, I check her decks and hull for signs of something amiss: a loose line, a dent or nick, bad trim telling of excess water in the bilge. All looks well. I grab a handhold on her long, overhanging boom and step on. With a Senior's low freeboard, it is barely more than a level step from the Whaler bow to the sailboat deck. She is heavily built, stable, and moves minimally and pleasantly in the water under my weight.

In a moment's time I tie off the Whaler and throw foul-weather gear and sandwiches below. It's blowing harder already. Creaking noises tell a story of the wind's strength. Even here in the inner harbor, the boats are pitching busily in the chop. West Bay is shoal – nothing more than a three-quarter-mile-square former meadow covered by thin water, with a six-foot-deep channel and various small mooring areas dredged out.

Sail stops are quickly undone with a pull on the loose ends of the half-reef knots. The big gaff main unrolls to the cockpit sole. I stand on the bench seat and look around while putting in the battens: not much activity this weekday morning. Classes are beginning at the club dock and the Beetlecats or, more lately, Optimist prams are loaded with kids. Crosby's tug is towing a beautiful blue Bermuda 40 towards her berth in Eel River. A couple of fishermen in work skiffs are clamming on the shoal inside the channel bend off Wright's Point. It is half-tide. A typical summer morning on West Bay.

I hank the picnic jib on and leave it lying loose on deck with the mooring buoy line thrown over so it will not blow off. Then, bracing my feet against the bulkhead, I grab the two halyards and haul up the main, keeping the gaff almost level until the sail is fully hoisted on the luff, then hoisting the gaff almost to its normal angle. The gaff peak will be hauled up further later as the halyards and sail stretch, but this will do for now.

I used to coil up the long halyard ends and stow them below, flat on the cuddy bench or hanging on a peg inside the bulkhead. Nowadays I leave them piled on the cockpit bench – a tip from an old fisherman who said they wouldn't kink if left as they fell. He was right. This makes a lot of difference when you are lowering the big mainsail in dicey conditions and want it down fast and smooth.

The jib hoists easily but then flogs, the clew shackle beating against the Sitka spruce mast where I have placed adhesive strips of protective material. I heard about a boat whose mast was so weakened by this beating that one day it fell like timber to the axe.

I walk the Whaler up and tie the painter to the mooring loop. Fortunately the boat is swinging away from those moored close to starboard, so I cast off hurriedly and hop back to the cockpit with all possible speed. I arrive just after the main sheet begins to run out, and I jerk it into the cam cleat on its block which secures it handily. I give the tiller a pull to keep her from heading up, and ease down to leeward to set the jib sheet in its cam cleat. Both ends of the jib sheets are tied together since I am alone today, and I bring the continuous looped line back with me as I finally sit down at the tiller. Under way.

The first puff stands the boat on her ear. Nearly dead in the water, a heavy mass, she converts the wind's force first to heeling moment, then slowly to forward motion. I climb happily out on the gunwale, hanging beyond it, sitting on the hull's side. I peer down at the boat's coppery red bottom and her long, shallow keel. We draw $2^1/_2$ feet, centerboard up; it stays up until we reach deeper water outside the cut, a matter of policy in the shoal depths of the bay.

Slowly the boat settles down, taking the wind, redirecting it with her sails, harnessing energy in the process, moving forward, heeling less. I climb in off the rail. The next good puff will send me out there again, exultantly riding this wildly-tilting platform.

I concentrate on staying clear of moored boats. One tack carries the first leg of the channel past Garrison's Point. The next series of tacks takes me down the main segment to the cut. The tacks are short, the dredged channel being only about forty yards wide, but tacking is easy. The looped jib sheet can be jumped out of its cleat, and the new one cleated with little fuss. The main sheet stays cleated. On a boat of this size, this weight, a cleated main will cause no problem provided it can be released quickly if necessary.

On the beat, puffs coming from the west over the high Oyster Harbors land heel the boat again. Solid water pours in over the coaming and runs out through the self-bailing scuppers in the cockpit. These are moments to remember: astride the high side, a foot hanging over the hull, much of the gaff mainsail

51

pressed well below eye level, a white wing curved against blue water, carving invisible wind. A shout pierces the rush of wind across the bay. Club kids in the small boats turn and laugh. Was that you?

Outside the cut, the wind has lightened a little and backed to the south. The Vineyard can be reached in one long tack. I settle in on a course for Oak Bluffs. The tide is going, as is said on Cape Cod, meaning going out. This gives me an extra two knots of speed over the bottom. In a two-hour sail, two knots means more than four miles added distance. Since Oak Bluffs is about ten miles away, this is a big boost. Better still, the tide will turn just before I start back; I will have it both ways!

The sun is hot, the breeze smells fresh, clean, salty. Off comes my shirt and soon, when I get clear of shore and neighboring boats, whatever other clothing feels unnecessary. I tie the tiller with a loose end of the backstay pull. The boat balances well enough to steer herself for a while. I lie down on the cockpit sole, grainy but smooth, warm teak against my back. With a hand free to adjust the self-steerer, I take my course from the masthead telltale and the feel of the boat. The white curves of sail all but blot out the sky, the water bubbles busily around the hull.

Near Succonnesset Shoal I sit up to look around. I will be there in another hour – it does not really matter where. The wind picks up and backs further to the south. I can now lay off for Oak Bluffs. The sailing is without problems but I must stay at the tiller, for my crude self-steerer works poorly on a reach. Two boats far to windward beat toward Edgartown. To leeward and ahead others round West Chop and harden up. They have a long beat to Edgartown against the last of the outgoing tide, whereas I reach comfortably past the breakwater, following the Hyannis ferry into the harbor at Oak Bluffs.

In the sheltered calm of the small circular harbor, I sightsee slowly among the moored boats. Three grizzled fishermen on the town landing watch. They appear curious about this gaff-rigged apparition ghosting through their harbor. When did a Senior last sail in here? A long time ago, to judge by their expressions.

I jibe in slow motion and buzz the dock, coasting in the light air. When we all have had a good look at each other, I head back out the narrow cut and set off on the return trip. It is a pretty harbor. Next time I will pick up a mooring and stay overnight.

On the way back the wind is further aft. I can broad reach. A fast point of sail and a following tide make progress rapid. I am past Succonnesset and Great Neck in less than an hour; in double that time I am running free up West Bay, almost too quickly home. I hate to see it end.

It has been a grand sail. Long after the last summer race is forgotten, I will remember it: the way the puffs off the Oyster Harbors shore heeled the boat, the sails against water and sky, the pleasure of going somewhere – anywhere – traveling effortlessly across the surface of the water, itself moving silently, rhythmically in great tidal surges.

·12·

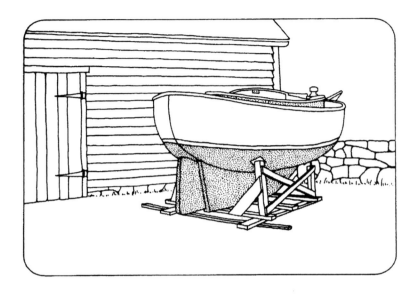

The Only Way to Buy a Boat

·

You do not pick a boat to buy. A boat picks you.

You declare yourself eligible, scout the boatyards, attend the boat shows, talk to anyone who will listen, and finally you meet a boat you cannot get out of your mind.

It will not do to skip the looking around. Not just at new boat shows and in old boatyards but from waterfront restaurant windows, along the docks, in harbors, in sailing magazines and classified ads and under winter covers. Somewhere inside you is a feeling for what a boat should look like. Finally you will find her.

Even if you have the spare cash to write a check for a shiny showroom beauty, I do not think you should do it. The boat would not be right for you. When you get to know it, hidden bad habits will surface. You will not spend much time together. You will eventually divorce.

Why so personal? For one thing, you trust your life to it. Reason enough. For another, boats are pretty. They have more compound curves than almost any other manmade object. When these are finely designed and built, a thing of beauty, even art, emerges: a Fyfe, a Herreshoff, a Crosby, a Frers, others.

Your boat may be of sound planking or Fiberglas and plastic or have an aluminum hull, in perfect shape. It may, on the other hand, need new paint, ribs, deck, rig, gelcoat – two years of backyard work before the first sail. Fine, if that is your pleasure.

Try to be sure you are in love, not merely infatuated. You are going to spend lots of time with her and a greater amount of money than you planned. You are trusting her to give you a lot in return.

Let me tell you how my boat picked me. We had taken a cottage on Cape Cod at Harwich Port during the month of July. We had three kids under the age of five. I wanted a boat to sail in, one in which I could take the two older kids along. I went searching for a charter. In Falmouth at MacDougalls boatyard, some forty miles away, I heard of a Wianno Senior for sale at Crosby's in Osterville. I backtracked fifteen miles or so and walked into Crosby's ancient main shed, stating my mission to Doug Higham, the wiry boat carpenter who stepped up the moment I entered.

"Well," said he, "we haven't got one for charter. Far as I know. 'Course you can ask Bill Crosby, up in the office."

I started up a narrow stair.

"You wanna' buy a boat?"

I came back.

"There's a Senior out there, sitting on the mooring. Just rebuilt her myself. New keel, new garboards, sheers, new deck – she's all new from the gunwales up. Ask Bill if she isn't good."

I did. Bill said he thought the boat was good as new. And he did not know of any boats for charter.

The next day I was on the way out to the mooring in Crosby's workboat for a trial sail. Innocent of the ways of these gaff-riggers, I had some amusing problems rigging; at least I assume they were amusing to the guys in the boatyard. On the second try I got the quadrilateral main on right side up. The wind was light north, dead behind me as I jibed under the drawbridge (giving myself half a scare, the space being narrow, the boom long) and ran down the channel. The boat seemed to sail herself, steady and pleasing in her motion.

I had not been sailing long in the Sound when another Senior came close, a man and a woman aboard.

"Want to race?" (Baseball cap. Anxious for a chance to pace with another boat.)

"Oh, I dunno. I'm kind of new at it. Trying her out."

"Well, if she can beat this boat, that'll be going some. This one's won the last seventeen races straight."

So I brought the rebuilt fifty-year-old boat close-hauled for a brush. No cigar. She would foot but not point with them. After three tries, they broke off.

By now we were a mile upwind.

"Try it downwind?" called I.

We sailed side by side in very light air, with little to choose between boats. Finally I slid over directly astern. I eased everything off and sat still.

Slowly the older Senior started riding up the other's stern. Before long, I angled onto his wind and sailed quite rapidly by. Wordlessly, the champion broke off and headed out into the Sound.

It was late afternoon, and my boat had picked me.

The next day the fleet champion had his boat hauled – perhaps looking for a flaw? And he did find Higham and asked if all the ballast weights had been put back into the older boat. The carpenter gave his assurances on that point, he told me later. But the champ may have been dead right. Some years later, after many seasons of going quite fast downwind in light air but hobbyhorsing slowly upwind in heavy air with a chop, it occurred to me to count the ballast weights myself. We were 120 pounds short – twenty percent of the inside ballast!

I asked the rebuilder-owner if I could take her out again with my family. They all loved the boat as much as I did. She sailed like a dream. Lots of room for the kids with an eight-foot cockpit and a cuddy cabin. Pretty lines. Brightwork aplenty. Teak cockpit sole.

Now came the eternal problem. A thousand hours of highly skilled labor had gone into the rebuilding. The price lay beyond my reach. I offered. Too little. Summer was marching past. Resigned, I chartered a Duxbury Duck in Wychmere Harbor. She was a cranky elbow-bumper of a boat; someone had altered her by placing a cuddy where there was room for none. Nonetheless the kids and I sailed her every day. We had fun but I thought often of the Senior. I heard that a man had bought her, writing a check on the spot for the asking price.

Two years passed. We took a cottage in Brewster near the sailing camp I had attended as a boy. I had heard that the man who bought the Senior lived in Orleans, a neighboring town. I asked around. None of my old sailing acquaintances could help. But at the town cove one dawn a friendly stranger told me he had heard of a Senior moored somewhere in Pleasant Bay and suggested I ask Jim Melcher, who ran a sailing camp over that way.

"Sure," said Jim, "I know the boat. It's up in Quanset Pond, kind of a hard place to find. Here's how you get there."

I found the pond at the end of a seldom-used dirt road off a little-traveled byway. I could never have discovered it without detailed directions. The pond was only one hundred and fifty yards across, and right in the middle – all alone – was moored the beautiful white-hulled Senior.

I borrowed a dinghy from the beach and rowed out. She had a new gold-leafed cove stripe to match her gold-leafed name on the quarterboard, and shiny brightwork. The cuddy was neat and stripped of excess gear. Lines were neatly coiled. Someone cared.

Next afternoon I was waiting on the beach as the new owner, Giles Wanamaker, along with his wife and a couple of grown children, hauled their dinghy up after a sail.

I summoned up nerve and introduced myself, telling of my own experience with the boat.

The owner was polite and seemed interested in talking about his boat. We chatted for a minute and he gave me his name and address before they left.

The following spring I wrote him a note asking that he please let me know if he were ever to consider selling.

Two days later I got a telephone call.

"How did you know I wanted to sell the boat?"

"I didn't."

"Well, it's uncanny. We just last week made up our

minds to sell."

"How much do you want?"

He named a figure below what he had paid. While I thought a second or two, he named another figure, lower. And said a new ouboard went with the deal.

"I want someone to have it," he said, "who'll care for her."

The following week I was at Arey's Pond boatyard at the appointed hour, checkbook in hand. The boat lay dockside, gleaming white, freshly painted, impeccably varnished.

We sat on a log along a beach road and I wrote the check. I felt him hesitate.

"Are you sure you want to do this?"

"No," he said. "But my wife does. I caught my foot in the mainsheet during a jibe last fall – pulled me almost out of the boat, the way she saw it. She made me promise to sell."

"I don't want to take it from you like that. Won't you talk to your wife again?"

He looked at me. I thought I saw mist in his eyes.

"No. I have to sell."

That Christmas, at his request, I sent him the gold-leafed quarterboard from her transom. Each summer I invited him to sail with us, but he never did. After two or three years they sold their house and moved to Florida.

And the boat, having picked me and arranged the unalterable circumstances of her purchase, shortly thereafter sailed me back to Osterville, her old home, my new one.

·13·

Varnish and Truth

•

Doing your own boat maintenance provides many pleasures. It gets you out of the house on the first warm spring days. It may bring you down to the water's edge if your boat is stored at a boatyard. There you will meet lots of other boating people, providing a nice chance to chat about the upcoming season and things nautical. If you live where boating continues all year you have plenty of time for maintenance, time that can turn out to be fun, as satisfying as sailing itself. It also gives you a more intimate knowledge of your boat and how it works. All the while, you save money.

Of course you may find it easier and great fun to write checks to the boatyard as the bills come in. As rates skyrocket, however, some people have suggested that the eventual function of many yards will be to rent space for the owner to work in, to provide expert advice, technical services and heavy equipment for haulouts, launchings and jobs that are too sophisticated for the individual to tackle.

Some yards will not allow owners to work on stored boats. Others impose restrictions: all work below the gunwales belongs to the yard, and boats whose owners do major maintenance will not be stored inside the sheds. The legality of restrictions is being challenged in some states.

By keeping the boat on your own property you avoid the problem. But few of us have adequate indoor shelter for our boats. Since certain boats definitely should be stored inside in hard climates, the boat owner would be helped a great deal if more boatyards could find a way to support owner maintenance and still make a fair profit.

Wooden boats belong inside. Rain seeps in, forms pools, and encourages rot and peeling paint and varnish. Sun dries the wood and the planks pull apart. A heated garage is worse than sun in its effect on wood. A shed with a dirt floor is best. It keeps the earth's moisture near the hull, retarding drying.

Wooden boats are protected by paint and varnish on every outside inch and on most interior surfaces too. Alternate freezing and thawing raises hob with the protective coatings. A wooden boat left in the water all winter suffers marked paint damage. Large flakes of paint peel off because of ice abrasion or temperature contrasts between the warmer water and frigid air acting on a hull soaked with water and condensation.

Lashing a canvas or plastic winter cover too tightly over

your boat can hurt more than help. One winter out boatyard built a new shed. All the Seniors in that yard were left exposed when the roof of the old shed was removed. (With beautiful Cape Cod frugality, it was used to roof the new shed, built to fit exactly under it.) Two boats were covered with canvas by the yard, as they were exposed longer than the others. Ours was one. The first warm spring day – at mid-April school vacation suddenly it was 85° – we came down to find heavy canvas covers pulled tightly over the boat, so tightly in fact that little or no fresh air could enter. When my son and I pulled the cover back, the temperature in the cockpit was surely over 100°, and the humidity was 100 percent. The trapped salt moisture in the boat's wood had been forcibly released, steaming the brightwork and paint as in a pressure cooker. At the oak coaming butts especially, vapor had worked under the varnish and raised an ugly, white, puffy blister that covered the blackening wood. I promptly lifted the bad varnish and refinished, but the damage can never be completely undone except by replacing the coamings.

The following winter our boat was at the same yard, still unfortunately stored outside. This time I covered it myself. I created large air holes at each end for ventilation. Having moved to Cape Cod year-round, I checked it weekly. Invariably I found that some of the yard personnel had collapsed the structure I had so carefully devised to preserve the air holes, and had rewrapped the cover tightly. The yards, even with the most helpful of motives, do make the occasional mistake.

Winter covers must allow for air to pass through. I think the best cover framework I ever saw was built of two-by-fours placed vertically to the ground at the boat's bow and stern. These were lashed firmly to the cradle-ends and to the boat. They were tall enough for the transverse two-by-four connecting them to clear all deck obstacles. A wide canvas was stretched over this frame and firmly tied. Its sides extended almost to ground level. The resulting shape was that of a pup tent with full open ends for ventilation. I watched that cover all one winter; it never ripped or chafed. The wooden boat under it looked fine in the spring.

Fiberglas – that is, glass-cloth-reinforced plastic – boats are in my opinion best left uncovered when stored outside. Covers seem to abrade and soil their topsides in the winter winds. Unless the boat has fine brightwork that needs protection, the cover serves little purpose. Plastic stands the weather well. Surely those who own small plastic sailboats and outboard hulls have proven this in their own backyards. In the spring a rubdown with gelcoat cleaner/waxer does the job, except on wood trim, which ought to be treated as on a wooden boat.

[The advent of shrink-wrap has modified my views. It doesn't flap around and abrade as do other covers. With care air can be allowed to circulate adequately. I have found after two seasons that shrink-wrap works so well on my wooden boat – with a proper ridge pole and wedges at the gunwales all around for ventilation – that winter storage outside leaves her in comparable shape to inside. On plastic or metal hulls shrink-wrap works very well.]

When spring comes, you can fit your maintenance chores to your skills and your pocketbook. Do what you can; enlist the boatyard for the rest. The people at the yard are the best source of advice on materials and techniques. Nothing can match their experience, their presence on the spot, their knowledge of local boat types and what works in local conditions. If you buy your materials at the yard shop and have the yard do the launching, hauling and more remunerative jobs, they are repaid for their advice. Usually they are glad to offer it. But be brief and listen carefully. Your conversation time may be charged to some other owner at a fancy hourly rate, but tomorrow may be turnabout!

In each yard you will find certain people from whom you receive clear answers that prove valuable. Other advice will seem unclear or will not pan out. The solution is obvious. The painter whose advice does not work for you may be the next guy's guru.

Plenty of books cover maintenance procedures. I have not found many as helpful as talking with knowledgeable boatyard people. But you do need a starting point, and a good book will serve if a yard is not available.

Finally, your growing experience will improve your work more than advice from any source. Like the yard, you will make mistakes. As elsewhere, mistakes are your best teachers.

I hope it will be helpful to touch on some of my own mistakes. The first time I varnished (except for Whaler seats and such) I chose a hot, brilliantly sunny day. We had a lot to cover and so kept working through the noontime sun. My older daughter, Deborah, then sixteen, helped. I wrongly instructed her to lay it on as thickly as possible without causing it to run. A better suggestion would have been as thinly as possible and still have it cover. Especially on vertical surfaces and especially for Deborah, who has a generous nature and likes to glop it on like paint. There are gloppers and go-lighters; you must learn to adjust your suggestions to suit.

Our thick varnish baked in the noonday sun. It dried all too quickly into interesting wrinkles and ridges, my introduction to "alligators" and "lace curtains." I had to scrape down, sand and start over on another day. Deborah pleaded a previous engagement.

That day we had tied the boat alongside the club dock to work. It was late June, the boat had gone in the water weeks before with the brightwork varnish undone (another mistake). Just as we finished the last touches on the coaming, an entire class of ten-year-olds debarked from their Beetlecats onto a nearby float. One splashed water at his friend; another did a picturesque cannonball at perilously close range. My temper sputtered, and I interrupted an enterprising plan to start a waterbomb war. But we now had waterspots decorating our alligators and lace curtains!

For years I had pretty good luck with Sigmavar, a Danish synthetic varnish. But after a while I began to raise hundreds of tiny air bubbles the size of BB shot. I switched to Z-Spar Captain's varnish. The bubbles continued. I talked to the boatyard paint crew. Nothing helped. Finally I discovered that I had developed a habit of removing excess varnish from the brush by sliding it against the lip of the bucket. That leaves little bubbles in the pooled liquid. The next brushload picks them up and they puff up on the finished surface in great profusion.

While wooding down brightwork and painted surfaces I have sometimes leaned too hard on the scraper, probably because it was not sharp. It then makes a deep scratch or lifts the grain of the wood, not easy damages to repair. Keeping a file handy and using it often will give you a sharp scraper.

I have varnished on very humid days. The finish comes out duller than you would like. Good varnishers have told me that they always try to varnish first thing in the morning on a dry day. I have found they are right. Varnishing outside after midafternoon is asking for trouble.

I once finished painting the deck in the evening after

supper. We had had a rainy spring and I wanted to get the boat in the water without further delay. All that season I sailed with certain sections of the deck, the "evening" ones, a mottled, dull version of the intended Grand-Banks-beige color. Evening dew does nothing for drying paint. I hate to think what it does to varnish.

I have, of course, made other mistakes. But, mercifully, I cannot recall them all at once. That is perhaps just as well for us both. You will learn from yours – and accumulate maintenance wisdom – better than from anyone else's.

·14·

Race, Anyone?

•

If you keep on sailing, sooner or later someone will ask you to race. The question is, should you?

The answer, I think, rests in human nature as well as cultural factors. Almost all people enjoy races and other competitive sports. But there are differences. The children of a certain Native American tribe always crossed the finish line of a footrace together; the swiftest simply waited for the slower children to catch up. In spirit everyone won by participating. This seems to me a lovely way to express and reinforce a spirit of community. It is not often found, however, in present-day sailboat racing. The racing bug that bites us seems to induce a fever which sometimes rises pretty high, a fever to win in the strict sense of placing first. Winners in our society do not often wait around even *after* they have crossed the finish line to greet losers. So if the bug bites, watch your temperature.

The scene plays something like this: you are sailing along in fine style, content with the peaceful pleasures of the day, when in the corner of your eye you see another boat, same class as yours perhaps – perhaps not – on the same course, not far away. You have to have a very saintly nature indeed not to notice which boat goes faster. Next minute you are tinkering a little to try to improve your boat's performance. The racing bug is tickling; soon comes the sting.

Racing, we hope, improves the breed, both of sailors and boats. It is fun too, if you win, or come in second, or place high in a competitive fleet. Losing, on the other hand, is said to be good for character and technically instructive. This is good news, because in racing fleets numbering twenty or thirty and more, only one boat can win each event, and not everyone sails as well as he might. We must conclude that an awful lot of character building and self-education takes place in the remainder of the fleet.

You can get hooked so hard on racing that you almost never take your boat out to sail except to race or to practice racing. Since racing effectively demands the highest concentration on a great array of technical details, you will probably forget to enjoy the sun, sea and sky. That's a pity. The evolution of the racing sailor, we hope, will not end in a mutation blind to the beauty of the silent sport's more philosophic pleasures.

Speaking of improving the breed, one wonders if the

notion is a tautology, self-serving the racing ranks. What breed are we improving? The speed breed – ever quickening the pace around the buoys but taking lightly such essentials as safety, good seamanship and fair sailing? Sometimes that seems to be the case.

We might as well admit up front the early speed-greed connection. The first international yacht races were often challenges sailed for large cash wagers and perhaps the prospect of increased business for the winning country's shipping industry. In fact the *America's* owners so hoped to lighten their British counterparts' coffers that they left instructions for her to be sailed slowly on her initial appearance in 1851 off Cowes, in order to entice larger bets. Sailor's pride got the better of wily scheming, however. In their first brush with the English, the *America's* captain and crew, including one of the owners who was aboard, could not resist the noble impulse to do their best. They sailed so fast that thousands of pounds of planned improvement in the younger country's balance of payments was skittered away. This discomfited *America's* other owners, who nonetheless subsequently won a nice big bottomless Cup through which millions of units of many national currencies have since figuratively flowed, redistributing huge chunks of the world's wealth from the rich into the pockets of skilled sailors and sailmakers, talented builders, gifted boat designers and inspired equipment makers, many of whom may well have started out in life poor and worthy.

Certain of the big spenders from abroad have reaped immense free advertising in the coveted American market by challenging for the Cup; an Australian real estate entrepreneur, a French pen and shaver manufacturer, an Italian high fashion house. The speed-money connection works in its own calculating ways. When you think about it, probably every hard-driving captain, from the early Phoenicians to the Cape Codders pressing every ounce of speed from their clipper ships, had market conditions in mind. The crew may have had other ideas. Not for nothing were the oversized sails that tugged impatiently from far-extended lower yardarms called studding sails.

As presently constituted, however, most sailboat racing involves outlays of money ranging from outrageous to sinful, with minuscule returns. Cash prizes are few and rarely are side bets substantial enough to qualify as a return on investment. We are looking at pride here, and perhaps a search for pure excellence, and glory as well.

The sport currently has very little commercial sponsorship. That may change. [It did, particularly with regard to the America's Cup and around-the-world and other ocean races.] Some European newspapers offer prizes for various transoceanic races. A beer company and a watch manufacturer have helped on occasion by sponsoring some United States racing. Professional racing may be on the near horizon. At present the hot sail lofts and design offices are exerting a lot of factory team effort, a la Grand Prix auto racing, to produce winners for the big spenders. This brings in other business. And of course the professionals argue, quite rightly, that the best improvements in equipment eventually spread. Not always, though. Paradoxically, marvelous innovations are sometimes outlawed because, it would seem, they threaten the value of large previous investments made by owners who carry clout in the rule-making bodies.

And so the reasons for wishing to make boats move more quickly get curiouser and curiouser. But the wish does exist and seems to occur in almost all of us if we scratch deeply enough. Still it may not hurt to bear in mind that a dedicated species of speed specialists may not be the most desirable end result.

For many small-boat sailors, the positive results of racing will outweigh the negative. Real advances occur in your knowledge of how the boat works, what makes it go, how to handle it in various situations. You study the wind with a much closer eye. You note and use minor shifts in its direction that a cruising sailor might leave unmarked. Weather becomes a close companion of your thoughts; you notice it carefully and you try hard to learn its patterns.

Racing is athletic. Pre-Olympic sailors now do bodybuilding exercises that compare with those in other sports. Hiking boards, weight lifting programs, jogging and other disciplines are used to build the needed strength. Agility and balance are important. Endurance is essential. Class boat racing at the higher levels can involve many consecutive eight-to-ten-hour days competing in extreme conditions.

In offshore boats this turns into days and nights on end. A high level of prolonged, concentrated effort is called for. In storm conditions your mental and physical energies may have to be devoted not only to the competition but also to saving your life or your companions or the boat, all possibly at risk.

Racing requires thought. It compares to playing chess while exercising on a tilted, moving platform under a cold shower. You need to think, and think calmly, in these conditions under close time-pressure.

On the other hand you get an unbeatable tan, plenty of exercise and lots of outdoor air.

Racing is social. You will meet other sailors, talk, compare notes, share common experiences. And post-race cocktail parties, awards ceremonies, meeting, dinners and dances are part of the fun, affording further chances to enjoy your colleagues' company.

On a personal level racing at every stage challenges you to do your best. When you do improve, you feel a growing satisfaction. The real fun may not come until the excitement of your first wins and high places, but the satisfaction of achievement starts early. With it comes increased self-esteem as a sailor and a person. Measuring up to the peer group, not necessarily winning, will nourish the spirit of almost every beginner. The inexperienced racer probably has the most to gain in terms of quantum leaps in his feeling for the sport, his knowledge and skills.

Every racing sailor has tales of races won or lost. The longer, more pathetic stories detail the losses. A listener, no matter how attentive, may have difficulty deriving the applicable lesson. I will spare you my racing tales in trust that you will go out and start working on your own.

I do recommend racing. But please do not go overboard! Some days are meant just for the pleasures of sailing, at peace and at one with the natural world around you. They are all too easy to give up, and very hard to replace.

·15·

Racing Hints for a Beginner

•

This chapter's subject might cause anyone familiar with my current racing record to raise an eyebrow. People who have beaten me regularly and grandly in recent years (almost everybody) may wonder if I am out of my depth. Of course, now that son Steve skippers the Senior, the record looks better. I am occasional crew, fiddling in the cockpit or wrestling manfully on the foredeck, trying to pass the time gainfully and not distract the skipper. Perhaps I should make this a crew piece.

Most recently I have taken to racing against the kids and a handful of adults in the weekend morning Beetlecat series or, more rarely, in Lasers. After nearly half a century I find myself back in really small small boats. And these pre-teens and teenagers can show you a thing or two! At least six from our club's program have won regional championships and placed high in national events. Several others have outstanding records. [Out of this group eventually came a world champion in J/22s, a college All-American, an America's Cup winning designer and other great sailing achievements.] They will soon have you talking to yourself on the race course.

Once upon a time, when I was in that age range, luck smiled on me. For four or five summers a long string of wins in our hard fought camp races went to and me and Gus Leinbach and Danny Byrnes – the best crew I ever sailed with. It seemed that in our local boats and home waters we could hardly lose, even to the occasional hot Edgartown Regatta winner who might drop in.

As a college freshman I brought to the team tryouts my unsophisticated Cape camp experience. At the end of a long, light-air day in dinghies I found myself on the four-man Yale sailing team. The other three were Bob Coulson of Marblehead, one of three double Sears Cup winners in the entire history of the sport; Bobby Monetti, a light-air genius from Manhasset, Long Island who ranked in almost every way with Coulson; and Dick Carter, who went on to win the Fastnet Race twice in boats of his own design, among other world-class sailing achievements. Carter crewed for Monetti, I for Coulson. From these three sailors I began to see how little I knew of racing. Largely through their talents the team won three national intercollegiate titles in four years.

In my junior and senior years I left the campus for the Middle East, spending part of 1948 serving in the Israeli War of

Independence and most of the 1949-50 school year preparing a senior Scholar of the House thesis on the kibbutzim there. I missed two sailing seasons entirely. The team did not seem critically hurt. When Coulson was graduated, Carter stepped in as B skipper and with Monetti won the nationals a second time and a third time. The preceding year they had a "bad" year, placing second. Prior to these heroics (their feat has never been duplicated in collegiate racing and probably never will be) I had pulled up the board too soon on one of Coulson's artistically hairy mark roundings and he had enlisted another crew – Ned Hayes – who had a firmer grasp of the phrase, "Not until I tell you!"

Then came graduation, the trek west as a journalist-for-hire, an exciting year with the Minneapolis Star-Tribune, three years part-time in the backroom mines on Wall Street supporting myself while trying to learn how to be a serious writer and then a family business in Massachusetts to run. During that period I raced a sailboat once on a lake in central Massachusetts and was nonplussed to find out that whatever touch I had had in small boats had gone with the wind.

Finally, twenty years out of dinghies, I was asked by a friend to help crew his family's lovely forty-four-foot cutter in an early spring race on Long Island Sound. The boat had been going badly for years, and his father, having visions of better days ahead, had recruited a rock-star skipper and crew. Two-thirds of the way down the first leg – a long, light air run – we were doing so badly that with painfully obvious desperation the helm was turned over to me. I had been cruising in larger boats the previous few years – not racing – and I had never felt a sweeter helm than this boat's. She just wanted to go, and with good fortune we began to pick up boats. At the leeward mark we rounded close behind the pack. On the beat the wind freshened. The helm was turned back to the professional upwind specialist. We climbed through the fleet and finally drew even with one of the front-runners, *Chee Chee IV*. Then the genny blew out. The number two jib went up. The main blew. Goodbye *Chee Chee*. Goodbye glory.

When I got our Senior my latent racing virus was artfully fed by the skipper of a tail-ender boat on the mooring next to ours. He was seeking a boat he could take points from, perhaps. After twenty-five years I came back to racing. As I have indicated, plenty of people have taken points from me since then – although not that particular skipper!

Such are my modest credentials that it seems plain I should not be giving extensive advice or "inside" tips on racing. Lots of books do, on different levels of expertise. What I would like to offer are a few hints for the skipper thinking of trying her racing luck.

Race at your own level if possible. Getting horizoned by a more expert fleet is a slow, painful way to learn. In fact, you do not learn when you are too far back of the pack, but you do normally get discouraged.

Recruit, and retain, good crew. That's the skipper's first and most important job. Racing is a team sport if the boat holds more than one. Sailing teams win, not the person at the helm, just as football teams win, not quarterbacks.

Sail. Sail a lot. Practice, too: mark roundings, timed starts, spinnaker sets and takedowns, tacks, jibes, the whole gamut. It is satisfying to do, and it will pay off on the racecourse.

Get the best equipment you can. Then forget it as a factor in the race. Equipment does not usually win sailboat races in one-design classes, where it is mostly standardized. Skill, cool-headedness, concentration, competitive spirit and yes, luck – which generally finds the ones best prepared to deploy all the above – do.

If your boat goes slowly, do not accept slowness as intrinsic to the hull. More likely the causes lie in your setup and tuning and the way you sail.

Most important, do not let the other sailor convince you that she owns a faster boat. This is unlikely in a one-design class. It is important psychologically for you to resist the very idea. She may have faster sails in given conditions, or set and trim them better, or do a number of things which give her hull superior speed. You can do those things. If you do them better your hull will probably go faster.

Learn wind shifts and the intricacies of water currents. Use them until doing so is second nature. More races are decided by these factors than any other except pure boat speed.

If tide is a factor in your race area, study the tidal currents religiously. Unfortunately it may take years to unravel local mysteries that are plain to competitors whose grandfathers have raced in these same waters, but unravel them you must.

Spend money chiefly on sails. They are your engines and you are in a speed contest. Learn to set a sail. Experiment. Pace against another boat, switching one sail, one control, at a time. Have the best sailmaker/racer from the loft where you buy, sail with you – if possible during a race – and pick his brain. Buy sails slowly, thoughtfully, but do buy them.

Tune your boat. Know your boat – a function of time spent sailing, and maintaining. Shroud tension, headstay tension – vary them and record the effects in different wind speeds. Simplify and place your gear effectively. Mast bend, rake and placement bear on the sails' ability to supply power. Experiment here too. Install cleats, cams, leads, winches yourself. No one at the yard can have your feel for their exact placement. Seconds gained in trimming lines translate into feet, or yards ahead during the race.

On the racecourse watch the pattern of the boats on the fluid "chessboard." Keep in mind that you are not racing the clock to the mark but the other boats. Find the front pivot point of the fleet going upwind, get on it if you can, and try to stay on it through all the wind shifts and tactical moves. The same downwind – where you can pick up a surprising number of boats.

Start in the front of the fleet. No matter what your boat speed, with practice and good timing you can do this, as starts are primarily made against the clock.

Read racing books that speak to your level of experience, not above, not below. Dr. Stuart Walker, an expert and prolific writer, is the name to remember. Sail, sail, sail. If you race with poor results, talk to successful skippers in the fleet. Ask questions. Some will answer gladly and frankly, but don't expect them to reveal *all* their hard-won knowledge. Then go out and sail some more.

Have fun doing it. If you do not, return to pure pleasure sailing.

·16·

A No-Sail Day

•

A hot, calm day. Noontime and still no breeze. The surface of West Bay is smooth. Only the wake of a passing powerboat stirs the placid water. Even the tide has gone slack at dead low. No rips swirl around the pilings and channel buoys, where on the flood and ebb the current presses. The water is midsummer warm and the sun can't heat up the land rapidly through the haze of the day. No sign of a thermal, nor of a new weather front. The night has been hot, airless. A good day to go touring and swimming.

I take a bathing suit and beach towel from the back of

the car. Steve is somewhere around, perhaps at Crosby's snack bar having lunch with the other yacht club sailing instructors. He will not want the Whaler. Deborah is a college junior working as a swimming teacher in East Hampton for the summer. Mark, a freshman-to-be, is a municipal lifeguard in the central part of the state, living at his mother's house for the summer, as is Polly, our youngest, who is practicing daily with her swim team. I have no lessons to give this windless day, and boat maintenance is pretty well caught up now that it is early August. The Whaler – and time – are my own.

I propose to take a tour around our three adjoining bays – an interconnected waterway of unusual scope and beauty. I will beach the boat, lie in the sun, and swim when the fancy strikes me. I know of plenty of places along the way, some hidden so well they become for the time one's own private coves and beaches.

I hop in the Whaler from the float alongside the dock, cast off painter and stern-line clip and start up the engine. With the throttle just past idle, I swing slowly out through the mooring basin in the wide shallows of upper West Bay. Some old-timers call this particular section South Bay. It lies mostly east and north of the main body of West Bay, connected by a broad opening between Garrison's and Wright's Points. It *is* south of North Bay, but on grounds that south should not lie northeast of west, I shall go on calling it part of West Bay. Perhaps a hundred sailboats moor here in two to seven feet of water. They range from twelve-foot Beetlecats to forty-four-foot sailing auxiliaries.

I soon arrive at the far end of the mooring area about two hundred yards from the dock, near the east shore where our Senior lies. I check the boat to see that all looks well. It does. I resist the temptation to go aboard, knowing that if I do I will putter and fix and straighten up while half the day slips by.

The Whaler's blunt nose is turned west toward the channel. Eel River is southward, a quarter mile long, about fifty feet wide with shoals along its banks but deep enough in mid-channel for a beautiful blue Bermuda 40 and a shiny white Hinckley yawl of about fifty feet to navigate. Both boats are tied alongside docks in front of their owners' houses, which are set well back from Eel River. This is a nicer place than its name conveys. Several picturesque boathouses and many docks line the water's edge. A one-hundred-yard wide sandy neck crossed by a road makes a natural causeway separating the end of the river from Nantucket Sound. Old-timers say that one day a southeast storm at the flood will break through here and isolate the big houses reached by the causeway from the easterly part of Wianno. Perhaps, though it did not happen in the great storm of February, 1978. Since it dead-ends so abruptly, I rarely go up Eel River. Today I pass its entrance by.

I often stand when steering a stable skiff or Whaler. So do fishermen and boatyard workers in their sturdy workboats. You can see better, move about faster, and cushion wave shocks comfortably. Easily capsized boats – dinghies, canoes, shells, some boardboats and small sailboats – present a tricky platform to stand on. So we normally ask beginners to sit down, equating sitting with safety. Having learned this lesson, people continue to sit down in larger boats that would not capsize under the weight of several persons standing on the gunwale. If the boat has good initial stability, standing is as safe and perhaps safer. I hold onto the painter or the stern line, or the wheel or tiller, for balance. In large boats, the helmsman rarely sits unless the boat is on a problem-free course. On ships, theoretically never.

Inexperienced passengers, on the other hand, should be

seated. They often lack a handhold and cannot anticipate which way, or how suddenly, the boat will move. The helmsman can see better if they sit, too.

In our Whaler I often remove the aft thwart, where the driver normally sits, to make better standing room. On straightaways I steer at low speed either by shifting weight from side to side or guiding the wheel – which is too low to reach otherwise – with my lower leg. The sensation is something like skiing gently down an easy slope. It is pleasant; I commend it to those with the proper boats.

So standing in the Whaler and steering with my leg, I pass at slow speed between Wright's and Garrison's Points into the wider, larger part of West Bay. On my right hand, between Wright's Point and the windmill at Oyster Harbors (Grand Island) gatehouse, lies the sandy southern shore of Little Island. At the end of this thousand-yard stretch – along which some ten or twelve big summer houses front – lies a little cove with about two feet of water at low tide. It extends almost to the windmill. Its banks are lined with eel grass higher than the water is deep. Two houses snugly hide in the pine grove along its shore.

A short causeway connecting Little to Grand Island separates this cove from North Bay. I could throw a stone over the causeway into North Bay from here, but traveling by water I will have to go three miles around Grand Island to reach the place where it would fall.

Leaving the cove and heading down West Bay, which is about a half mile wide, the shore of Grand Island is on my right. Water depths between the mid-bay channel and the beach are one to three feet at low tide, though sub-channels with slightly more depth can be found near the shore. Along the Grand Island high ground, about a half-mile stretch, is another line of ten substantial summer homes. The last group of four houses belongs to a famous American family who founded and gave its name to a pre-Revolutionary War munitions, now chemical, corporation. They sit on a small peninsula that juts into the junction of West Bay, Mellon's cove, the Seapuit River and the Osterville cut – the Times Square of our watery highways.

On the left past Garrison's Point lies the sandy shore of Wianno, a posh seaside section of Osterville village. Set back on its slope are five or so spacious homes, each with its acreage of manicured grounds. Toward the mouth of the channel the water on this side of the bay thins out in places to three or four inches – sometimes bare sand at low tide – though with local knowledge you can find a tricky six-foot-deep sub-channel near the shore. Here the tip of Wianno angles back toward the center of the bay, almost enclosing its southern end. The land is lower, with stately residences. The last stuccoed, sprawling house looks across a two-hundred-yard gap at the mouth of West Bay and down the Seapuit River.

As the Whaler glides through the bay's mouth, I have several choices. By turning right I can follow the narrow Seapuit River, not really a river but a saltwater connector between West and Cotuit Bays, a sort of inland waterway. It divides the southern sandy shore of Grand Island and a thin island-dune known as Dead Neck or – at its Cotuit Bay extremity – Sampson's Island.

If I go straight out through the Osterville cut into Nantucket Sound, I can proceed around the outside of Dead Neck-Sampson's Island and reenter the bay system at Cotuit. One can beach the boat and swim on either side of Sampson's. The Audubon Society has managed the fragile island-dune since the donation of the land as a bird sanctuary by residents of Grand

Island. Access is limited to Society members and village residents holding permits. The bird population consists chiefly of gulls.

I turn into the Seapuit River. The hot afternoon has brought picnickers and swimmers to Dead Neck. Their boats are anchored or beached. On the right bank of the river Grand Island passes by as I embark on the second leg of its circumnavigation. Along Grand Island's Seapuit shore are grand houses, only about fifteen in a mile-long stretch. Most have solidly built docks with solidly built boats tied to them.

The gulls across the river – which is thirty-five yards wide at low tide and ten more at high – nest and chatter and hatch their young in a somewhat more raucous manner than their neighbors on the opposite shore, the donors of the sanctuary. These benefactors have benefited themselves, not entirely accidentally, by limiting beach traffic near their homes, protecting a natural barrier to their beachfront from overuse and removing the property not only from tax rolls but also from the reach of an unsuitable purchaser.

On breezy days it is great fun to sail through the Seapuit. The southwest wind comes with full force over Dead Neck, heeling your boat, but the water remains smooth as a rippled pond, protected from waves by the dune barrier. Today, breezeless, the normally cool Whaler floor feels hot to bare feet. I begin to think of a swim. I throttle up a little to the no-wake speed limit. Emerging from the river I cross the southeastern corner of Cotuit Bay. I swing out through Cotuit cut and around to the outer side of Sampson's Island. After a few hundred yards I anchor and step onto the beach.

Not a person in sight. Heat waves shimmer off the sand, too hot to walk comfortably on. I hop up the beach to a hollow in the dunes and sunbathe. Soon perspiring, I run for the water and dive in. The drop-off here is steep – ten feet out the water is over my head – which is not true of any but this stretch of Sampson's Island. The water is about 70°, pleasantly cooler than the air, which must be over 100° above the sun-heated sand. The swimming is perfect.

After an hour of swimming and sunbathing I climb – wet, cooled and happy – into the Whaler, towel off and resume my tour. The channel crooks around Sampson's through Cotuit cut, bends past Bluff Point – one massive, ancient vacation castle looming on its height and several contemporary palaces on the slopes nearer the beach – and then into Cotuit Bay. At $1^{3}/_{4}$ miles, Cotuit Bay is longer than West Bay and wider. The picturesque village of Cotuit sits on its western shore – a lovely white church spire, a cluster of traditional Cape gray shingled houses and a sturdy town dock just visible through the masts of several hundred moored sailboats.

The water in mid-bay is as much as sixteen to twenty feet deep, far deeper than West Bay. In the 1800s and early 1900s coastwise schooners entered through Cotuit and sailed up North Bay as far as Osterville landing near the foot of Bay Street, there unloading cargoes of coal and bulk goods. On the right hand as they tacked through Cotuit Bay was a forested Grand Island, known as Hannah Screechum Island after Captain Kidd's Native American consort. Local legend says that he murdered Hannah and buried her body on the island so her ghost would protect his hidden pirate treasure. Nowadays the island's shore shows glimpses of summer homes hiding among the trees, and is beach-lined. Kidd's treasure has never been found, but the real estate owners and developers harvested a far greater one.

On the left hand traveling northward one sees houses

generously spaced along the wooded bluff overlooking Ropes Beach and its serene cove. Here are more moored sailboats and, as the bay opens out again beyond Handy's Point, the dock and two gray shacks of the Cotuit Oyster Company, which harvests the most delicious oysters from its grant beds in the bay shallows. Here too is a cozy cove with a mooring area of perhaps thirty small boats, mostly sail.

In Cotuit and North bays during World War II the army engineers and Coast Guard trained amphibious landing craft operators for D-day and the Pacific landings. Two camps were set up, named with whimsical Cape Cod humor in the spirit of the times: Camp Canduit in North Bay and Camp Havdunit at Crosby's boatyard in Osterville. One Cotuit historian recalls that the beach was blacktopped from the oyster company up to the Narrows to facilitate the operation. Practice landings were made on Dead Neck and other beaches further west on Nantucket Sound at Waquoit and Popponesset.

Beyond the oyster company for the next half-mile a passage – the Narrows – leads into North Bay. The schooner skippers bound for Osterville must have needed patience and cunning to sail through. High hills line both banks, between which the gap is only about 150 feet; winds are fluky; the buoyed channel is hardly more than 50 feet wide and 6 feet deep today. It has shoaled some over the years, but can you imagine sailing a 60-foot cargo schooner in – engineless, full-laden and shorthanded, with only a deckhand and a cabin boy to help? Perhaps this kind of training helps explain why Cape Cod and Nantucket captains were top guns in the expanding 19th century American merchant fleet and won respect 'round the watery world, whaling and trading.

Passing out of the Narrows I stay in the marked channel

for another 250 yards. A 2-foot shoal lies on either hand at low tide. Then North Bay, almost a perfect oval, three-quarters of a mile long by one-half mile wide.

Here is the hurricane hole for some of the Cape's most valuable boats. Some two dozen hollow steel balls about six feet in diameter glower on its surface – hurricane moorings for the larger yachts. Other boats – several hundred come in during a good hurricane scare – merely anchor within the bay's protection. It is nearly two miles inland from Nantucket Sound. Its shores are sandy, again discreetly lined with houses. At its north end the little Marstons Mill river curves a quarter mile through eel grass banks and hidden marshes to Prince's Cove, a smaller, muddy-bottomed mooring area and storm refuge. Dam Pond, Bog Pond and Ishem Pond indent North Bay's northeast shore, all but Dam Pond too shoal for navigation except by canoe or skiff. On the opposite side of North Bay a pretty cove extends about five hundred yards to the causeway near the Oyster Harbors gatehouse, over which I could have thrown a stone at the trip's start.

North Bay is a designated water-skiing area. This afternoon, with no wind and hot sun, two or three skiers are out – a crowd as things go in North Bay. The sport always looks dangerous to me. As a boatman I see some potential for one ski boat in a closed area to hit another at high speed while both drivers are distracted by the business and excitement of towing a skier. The rules require each boat to carry a second person as observer to discourage the driver from looking back, but he looks back anyway at times. The big steel hurricane buoys create a hazard, as do miscellaneous other boats traversing the bay. I give the kids in the ski boats a wide berth, heading into the channel that will take me under the bascule bridge back into

West Bay.

This channel leads through low-lying land left and right to a boat basin about five hundred yards long. The docks and slips of the two Crosby yards line its edges. In the middle of this basin, which is about two hundred yards wide and is often called simply "the river," are moored some large sailing auxiliaries. Large and mid-sized motoryachts are slipped at docks and floats lining the shore. The two boatyards are a source of never-ending interest, providing a seasonal spectacle of comings and goings, of big boats and small, local boats and visitors from far ports, spring launchings and fall haulouts, and the painting, repairing, carpentry, rigging and plain ingenuity that go into caring for the boats. Many older, beautiful wooden boats sail from here, as do reinforced plastic and metal ones. Wooden boats are occasionally built and often rebuilt in the Crosby sheds, as craftily as ever. Plastic hulls are sometimes built or finished out nicely in wood. The nature and expertness of the work done at both yards commands attention. The first Crosbys started to build boats along these shores in about 1800. The boats they built are known and respected throughout the sailing world.

Just past the Crosbys the river narrows to sixty feet and flows beneath the bascule bridge. I pass under its twenty-one-foot central span into West Bay against a flooding tide that sluices around the pilings. On the right bank is Joe Crosby's picturesque oyster shack, motif #2 (the one at Rockport Harbor is #1) for New England artists. Several fishing skiffs are tied up in front. [Today, unfortunately, Joe Crosby's shack has given way to three or four elegant summer homes, and the fishing skiffs replaced by a powerful, shiny sport fishing yacht.] Then Wright's Point again, and opposite, on the left bank, the club dock.

I tie up the Whaler. I have motored almost five miles while only once retracing my route, spent three delightful hours, had a swim at an isolated beach – yet just skimmed the surface of these wonderful bays, cuts, rivers, coves, ponds and channels. It takes many a no-sail day to know them well.

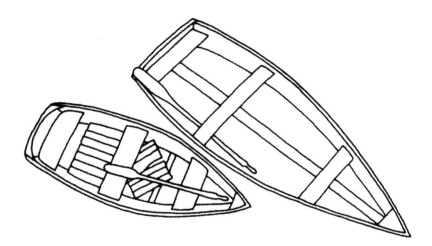

·17·

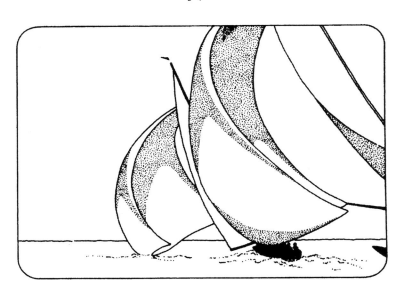

Sails

•

Sails are so beautiful that analyzing how they work seems altogether unpoetic. Furthermore, experts disagree on the answers to some questions and on the emphasis on certain factors. The inquiry becomes a chase and puzzle. Carefully thought-out theories do not always work especially well when actually applied to building faster sails. Then some sailmaker's intuitive or accidental new wrinkle results in the fastest sail in the fleet. The scientists sit down ex post facto to figure out and explain why. Eventually we have a modified, improved, even brilliant theory. Its sanctity lasts until the next evolutionary leap.

Progress may not always happen that way. But it happens often enough that you can remain healthily skeptical of any theory you read about sails, including what appears in the following paragraphs. Less is known than written.

[In the past twenty years, since the above was written, the exponential increase in use of high technology has given sailmakers a more accurate understanding of fluid dynamics – in this case the way moving air acts upon a sail. Cad-cam, laser-cutting machines and other new hi-tech tools can translate knowledge into precise sail shapes. New materials like mylar and kevlar help keep the shapes stable when stressed. But the sailmaker's intuition and art will still produce the occasional inspired breakthrough, and will in any case affect the final result.]

A sail set wide to catch the wind from aft transmits force from the push of the wind on the presented side, moving the boat downwind. Simple as that. Or is it?

If the wind is piling up against a wide-set sail's facing surface, it creates higher pressure against that surface than on the back side. The lower atmospheric pressure on the back side therefore sucks the sail forward. Not, as we first thought, the push on the front surface. Right? (diagram p. 92: **Air flow around sails: running free**)

Yes right, although I am not sure you have said anything very beneficial or uplifting when you have said this. When the pressure increases on only one side of the sail, it becomes relatively lower on the other. In a simpler age, we might have been content to ascribe the moving force to the push and ignore the pull, rather than articulating the force as "pressure differential."

But this is not a simpler age. For instance, here is an

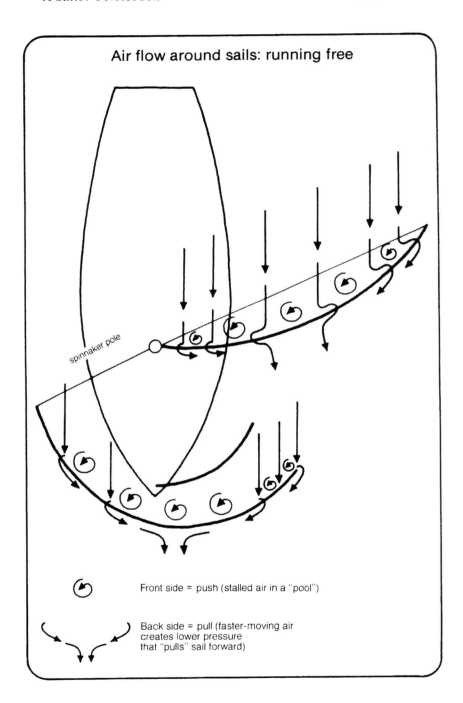

Air flow around sails: running free

spinnaker pole

Front side = push (stalled air in a "pool")

Back side = pull (faster-moving air creates lower pressure that "pulls" sail forward) odd fact: bag out a mainsail on a run on a light day, and it will go faster than a flat sail. But, bagged (i.e., bellied to maximum curve by easing outhauls, downhaul, other controls), the sail actually presents less surface area for wind to push, since it is not stretched so far on the spars. The boat might be expected to go slower. But it does not.

The nice, curved backside is thought to cause this oddity. Air seeping around the edges of the sail runs along it like syrup over a pancake. That is the nature of air, it acts like a fluid. After curling around the edges of the sail, it flows along the backside faster than the air that is pooled and slowed in the belly of the baggy sail. Air going faster over one side of a surface creates even lower pressure on that side, the physicists tell us. The pressure differential, transmitted from the sail-rig to the hull, produces motion.

Finally the air detaches from the backside curve, delaminates as the flow analysts say, and goes on its hastened way. This process continues throughout the life of the flow.

The famous example usually given is an airplane wing. Because it is curved on its top surface and flatter on the bottom (you can check next time you fly), a wing lifts. At least so we are told. If that is so, how can stunt planes fly upside down? I can only refer you to the aeronautical engineering and flow analysis books. And remind you about skepticism when confronting a single, all-encompassing theoretical explanation.

I took as an extreme example the sail set wide for running free. The backside pressure differential may be clearer if we consider a close-hauled sail. May be.

The breeze strikes the sail's leading edge at an angle of around forty-five degrees. (If you are lucky enough to be sailing a Cup defender, at perhaps thirty degrees or less, but normally boats cannot sail that close to the wind's direction.) The sail shape is curved, of course. The *depth* and *placement* of maximum curve – the *chord* and the *draft* – can be decreased or increased and moved around by means of the outhaul, downhaul or Cunningham, mast bend, boom bend, shroud tension, cutting and sewing of sails and other means.

The wind divides around the mast and the sail's leading edge. Some goes around the backside, some across the front. We learn from theory that wind traveling the backside curve must speed up to reunite symmetrically at the sail's trailing edge with its sister breeze that traveled a "shorter" route on the front side. The resulting higher relative airspeed helps create lower pressure on the backside. Pressure differential goes to work, producing the sail's drive.

This is pretty well-accepted theory. It must be generally useful and I certainly do not want to meddle with well-enough. But did you ever see a cloth sail, even a Kevlar/mylar one, that had a flatter curve in front than in back? The wind on the front side follows a concave curve, just as the sister wind around back clings to the matching convex one. Then why would the divided breeze travel unequal distances at differing speeds over our sail "wing"? Lives there a sail designer who can create a soft sail that has a greater chord on one side than the other? (diagram p. 95: **curvature of sails**)

Hold on a minute. Look at the box kite: flat, spaced surfaces joined by a light frame. Flies like a bird. Like an airplane wing. Like a sail. Wins prizes at the kite picnic. And not a curved surface on it!

Maybe the kite's tail gives it flying ability. As a matter of fact, yes. Go figure. We'll come back to this later, we have to talk about sails now.

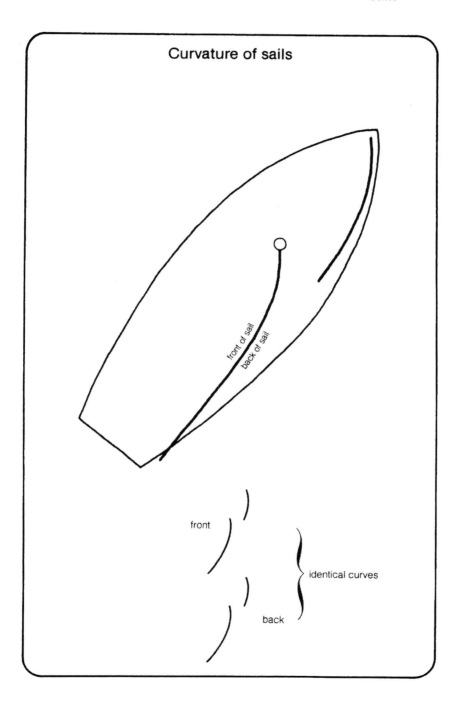

Curvature of sails

front of sail

back of sail

front

back

identical curves

Air moving across the sail's front side when close-hauled is slowed by turbulence in the pocket created by the chord, as in the case of the sail running free. The scoop or pocket shape on the front side alters and slows flow as does – importantly – the mast itself. Less impeded backside air would then have to move faster, and perhaps even travel a greater distance, as in the case over the airplane wing's top surface, to reunite with its divided component at the trailing edge. A pressure differential forms. The slot effect helps.

The sail "works." (diagram p. 98: **Back-side low pressure at work on a sail: close hauled**)

But what about the fellow flying in his upside-down stunt airplane? The curve of his wings faces the ground. The flat side points skyward. The air must travel further, therefore faster, across the wing on the curved side and "lift" the plane in that direction. According to our theory then, he should plummet to earth, since his wing's "lift" is working in reverse!

Back to the drawing board. Newton's third law holds that for every action there is an equal and opposite reaction. When the wind strikes a sail, air changes direction. The reaction to this change is equal and opposite: the sail tries to drive the boat in a direction opposite to the bisector of the angle of change. The boat's hull and keel convert this chiefly sideways but slightly forward thrust into forward motion. In my opinion this is the chief force acting to drive a close-hauled sailboat forward. It has more to do, in other words, with the angle of attack than pressure differential caused by curved shape. (diagram p. 99: **The chief force driving a sail: equal and opposite reaction to change in the wind's course**)

We must still give fair credit to pressure differential, although I think it contributes less than many sailors believe to the *vector* (defined as a mathematical calculation combining the direction and magnitude of forces acting on the sail, stated as velocity in a single direction and magnitude).

The sideways vector is converted to forward motion by the shape of the boat's underbody, as mentioned above. Otherwise sailboats would go mostly sideways when close-hauled. Sail close-hauled in a flat-bottomed centerboarder with the board up. You will see how much the sail's vector acts sideways and therefore how much the boat sideslips instead of moving forward.

Now perhaps we can satisfactorily ascribe to the wide-set sail with which we began this chapter its component forces. The chief force is pressure – a reaction to the blocking of the wind's free passage. The *pressure differential* component caused by curved shape provides a small increase in the strength of the vector. But as racers well know, a small increment is not too insignificant to help produce victory, if rightly courted.

We have not discussed the forces on sails while on a reach. I believe you can extrapolate. No one really knows all the answers. You may come up with something new and reach faster and better than us all.

We also have not discussed apparent wind, a result of the boat's forward motion. Put your hand out of a moving car's window. You feel artificial wind: wind created by the motion of the vehicle. Its direction is always from directly ahead, since this artificial wind comes from the car's forward motion. In a moving boat this artificial wind modifies the angle at which the natural wind strikes, bringing the direction from which this *felt* wind comes – the *apparent* wind as it is called – slightly forward. The *apparent* wind denotes the direction of the wind as it strikes your sail, taking into account the boat's forward speed.

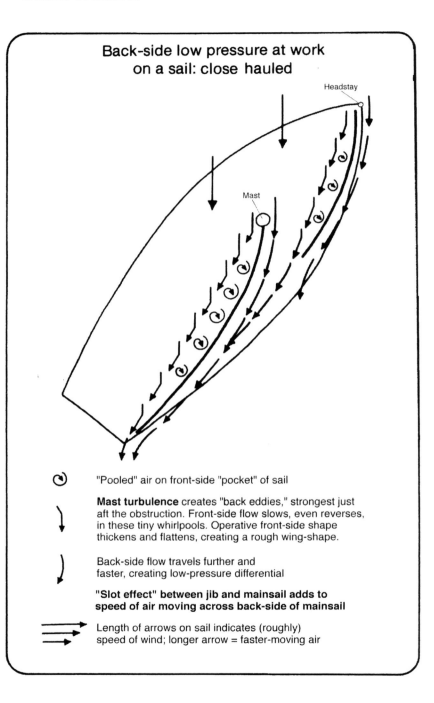

Back-side low pressure at work on a sail: close hauled

Headstay

Mast

(⟳) "Pooled" air on front-side "pocket" of sail

Mast turbulence creates "back eddies," strongest just aft the obstruction. Front-side flow slows, even reverses, in these tiny whirlpools. Operative front-side shape thickens and flattens, creating a rough wing-shape.

Back-side flow travels further and faster, creating low-pressure differential

"Slot effect" between jib and mainsail adds to speed of air moving across back-side of mainsail

Length of arrows on sail indicates (roughly) speed of wind; longer arrow = faster-moving air

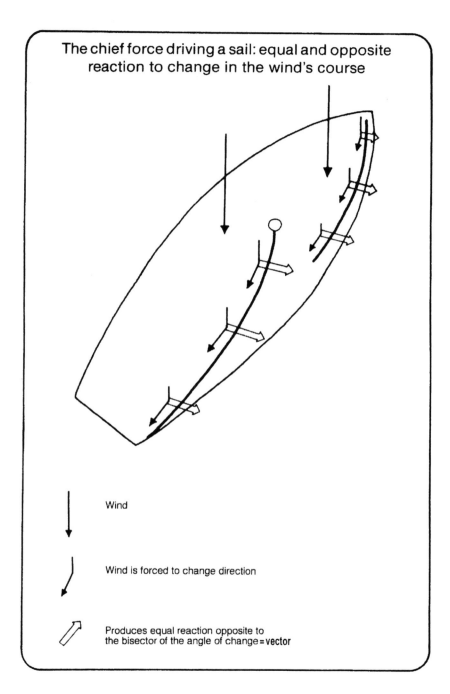

The chief force driving a sail: equal and opposite reaction to change in the wind's course

Wind

Wind is forced to change direction

Produces equal reaction opposite to the bisector of the angle of change = vector

The sail will act as if a little closer to the wind than you would have expected – or quite a lot closer if your boat is a fast one. It is useful to bear that in mind, but it does not change the basic nature of the forces driving a sail. (diagram p. 101: **Apparent wind**)

We also have not peered into the nooks and crannies of much sail lore, including the *slot effect* – the compression of wind in a multi-sail boat caused by the narrow gap between sails, forcing the air to accelerate like water in a sluice. This significantly increases the pressure differential on the backside of the trailing sail (viz., the mainsail in the diagram **Backside low pressure at work...**).

Or consider the wondrous efficiency of the Chinese junk rig.

But hold on. We have to stop somewhere.

Before we do, let's see if we can discover what keeps the upside-down airplane flying. The pilot keeps the plane's nose above horizontal. The reaction from the wind's redirection by the upward-angled wing *(the angle of attack)* holds the plane aloft, despite the curve of the wing's (temporary) underside. The wing does not lift as efficiently as if right side up. Nor can the plane go quite as fast. But it does fly.

So does the Chinese box kite, whose tail angles the leading edges of its flat surfaces upwards, forcing the breeze to strike the underside. *The angle of attack* produces the correctly lifting vector here too.

Now, how about a nearly flat sail made of metal or composite material, a so-called "hard wing" sail? Nope, not here, let's leave that to the hi-tech guys. They're working on it, believe me, and a lot of other esoteric stuff too; e.g. a rapidly-spinning vertical tube, which looks like the thick metal spine of a

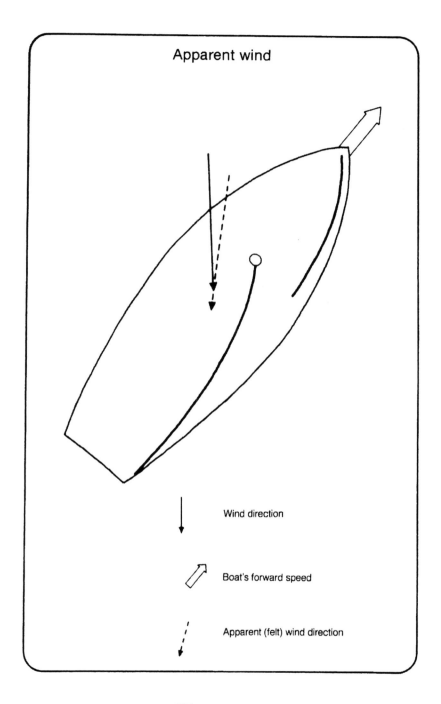

Apparent wind

Wind direction

Boat's forward speed

Apparent (felt) wind direction

whirling amusement park ride, and stands in place of the mast. How does it pull the boat forward? Well, the rapid spin induced by wind striking the rotor theoretically, we read, creates a pressure differential on the front side and presto, forward motion.

See what I mean?

·18·

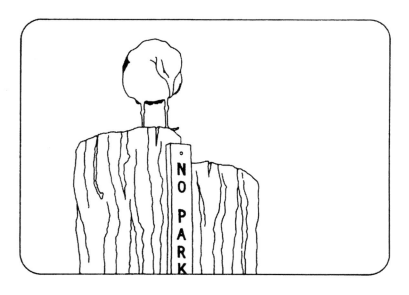

Wind and Calm

•

One summer morning you arrive at the dock early. Gulls are sitting placidly on the pilings. The water is flat. Mooring lines sag. Nearby boats point in opposite directions; the tide has divided into a main stream and a back current. No wind.

But you want to go sailing. Will the wind come up? The weather forecast will not really help you decide; it is not very accurate for local wind conditions.

The thing to do on a hot, sunny day in summer is wait. Periods of flat calm do not often last long in summer in our area. Where water and land meet, the significant temperature difference between hot, sun-heated land and the cooler water causes thermals, rising columns of hot air. When the hotter air over land rises, it sucks in a breeze from the ocean.

In New England, when the Cape and vast forestland of Maine to the northeast start to heat rapidly under a July sun, the thermal can draw in twenty-five knots of southwest breeze after a morning's dead calm. It will blow from seaward across Nantucket and Martha's Vineyard, cross the twenty-five-mile Sound and the Cape, and travel three or four times that distance over Cape Cod and Massachusetts Bays until it brushes the Maine coast. Finally over the inland heated forests it starts an upward rise. Even on days when the circulation in a high pressure system adds little impetus, this thermal blows strongly.

Later in summer, haze and low cloud may obscure the sun. Its angle is also lower in the sky. The land will not heat so rapidly. The water has warmed to 70° or more, further cutting the temperature differential. A faint southerly wind may result from a stagnant low pressure system to the southwest. Under these conditions, the thermal may not come in at all or may come less strongly and later in the afternoon.

In any case our local experience tells us that a dead calm will not last longer than an hour or two. That is why I do not give up on the day's sail quite yet.

You will learn to recognize the conditions in your locality that bring a new breeze out of the calm. When it is a half mile or so away you will see signs of the breeze approaching: dark ripples on the water's mirrored slick, sailboats moving in the distance, flags, clouds. With experience you can predict the time of the wind's arrival fairly accurately. Sharpen your observations and you will also become good at predicting the direction and strength of the new breeze.

If you go down to sail well into the afternoon and still find a dead calm in our area, it is probably the day to catch up on maintenance. Look for signs of a thermal or a new weather front. If you do not see any, start for the locker or the marine store. After all, the sun has had plenty of time to heat the land. If no breeze has come up yet, the chances do not look good that one will. What you would like now is a high or low pressure system to arrive, bringing within its circulation steady winds. These systems are normally accompanied by major shifts from the preceding wind direction and by a basic change in the weather. Forecasts predict them more accurately than they do local thermals. Sometimes you can step outside and almost feel the change coming.

The systems are several hundred miles in diameter. They are themselves partly confluences of thermals. Low pressure systems form when masses of warm southern air rise. In this hemisphere, air in low pressure systems rotates counter-clockwise. Warm, rising air lowers atmospheric pressure at ground level: hence, a "low pressure" system. The organized system is borne across the United States in a basically west-to-east upper airflow, the jet stream, sometimes curving and dipping north and south. The lows tend to travel north and eastward from southern warmth; the highs south and eastward from Canadian cool. The winds we feel as part of a low pressure system carry clouds and often precipitation, since the moisture in warm air rises high enough to cool and condense in the upper atmosphere and condensed moisture returns to earth as rain.

Cold, heavy air eventually falls downward to earth, raising atmospheric pressure at the surface and forming a "high pressure" cell. This air is relatively devoid of moisture, and in descending it warms and dries further. High pressure systems

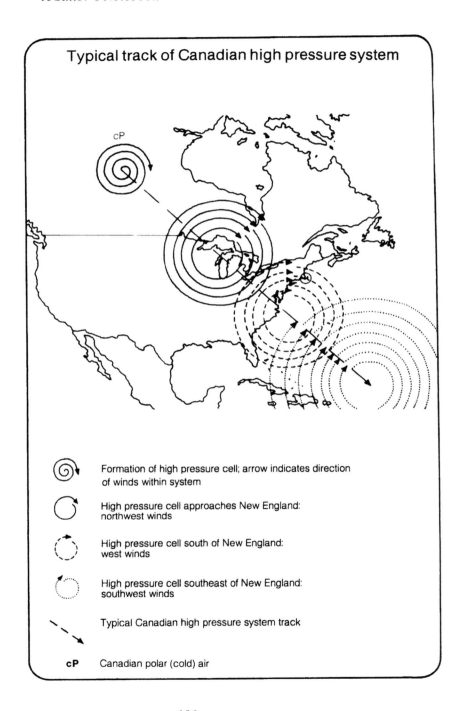

Typical track of Canadian high pressure system

Formation of high pressure cell; arrow indicates direction of winds within system

High pressure cell approaches New England: northwest winds

High pressure cell south of New England: west winds

High pressure cell southeast of New England: southwest winds

Typical Canadian high pressure system track

cP Canadian polar (cold) air

rotate clockwise in this hemisphere. The highs contain clear, dry air. They will bring first northwest, then west, and finally southwest winds if the center of rotation passes to the south of you, as it often does in New England. (diagram p.106: **Typical track of Canadian high . . .**)

The pressure systems are the huge factories of weather and wind. When they and the local thermals are both stagnant, it is a rare day in our area. A calm one. Not for sailing.

If you are caught out on the water in a breeze that drops dead, relax and enjoy the interlude. Lie on deck. Watch how the tide or current moves your boat – useful information for the future, especially if you race in these waters. Look at the sails hanging in repose against the sky. You will remember some of these quiet moments with fondness as among the best in sailing.

Of course you can trade such moments for an auxiliary power package: an outboard, gas tank, gas-oil mix, funnel, spare shear pin, a battery, extra starter pull cord and spark plugs. Then you can do what the inboard-powered auxiliary cruising sailboat almost invariably does: start the engine and not only shatter nature's calm but quite possibly your own, either through the noise and fumes when it does start or your frustration when it does not.

If your boat is small and you have the experience to maneuver in crowded harbors without auxiliary power, try to leave the outboard engine at home or mounted on the dinghy. It takes up space, makes noise, uses energy and deprives you of what nature and life rarely offer – calm.

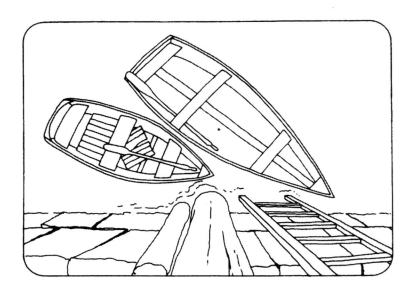

Tide

•

Here on Nantucket Sound the tide rises and falls as predictably as the moon revolves about the earth. Tide in our harbor takes 6 hours and 12 minutes to come in. And about another 6 hours and 13 minutes to go out.

Two cycles take about 24 hours and 50 minutes. So tomorrow afternoon's high tide will occur about fifty minutes after today's. Tide peaks at 1:00 P.M. today, about 1:50 P.M. tomorrow, 2:40 P.M. the third day and roughly so on.

Tide is strange. It seems a simple phenomenon – everybody learns that it has something to do with the moon's motion and gravity – but is quite complex. At Boston it rises anywhere from eight to twelve feet going from low to high, ebb to flood. The wide range occurs because of the changeable positions of the moon and the sun with respect to our planet. Tide height is also affected by passing low pressure systems: low pressure on the water's surface allows the water level to lift; high pressure inhibits it. That is one reason why a storm, which accompanies a low pressure system, presents special flooding problems along the coast.

Tide is not the same around the globe. In the Caribbean Islands the normal rise is less than two feet from low to high. Nor does it peak there every 12+ hours; it peaks only once every 24+ hours (called a diurnal, rather than a semidiurnal tide). Strangers in the Caribbean often cannot tell when high tide occurs, or if the tide has changed at all.

A few hundred miles north of Boston in the Bay of Fundy, where the water enters a wide-mouthed dead-end funnel, the tides at the far end climb fifty feet against the shore. At Inchon, South Korea, forty feet. Along the English Channel's coastline, almost as much. But in the Mediterranean, as in the Caribbean, the tide is hardly noticeable.

Strangely enough, many sailors have an amazing lack of knowledge about the tides. Just last summer a young man I know who has sailed intensively and raced successfully for fourteen years was surprised to find out that the highs and lows come progressively almost an hour later each day in our area. He had not noticed!

I am not an oceanographer or meteorologist, you will note. Wisdom would dictate that I maintain silence on so technically complex a subject as the operation of the tides – leave this section of the chapter blank, in other words. At the urging, however unwisely, of my editors, I will try to set out a few floating bits of information – and then as quickly as possible get on to talking about how sailors find practical use for tides.

The moon's gravitational attraction contributes to the creation of tide. To a lesser extent, so does the sun's. When they both line up so as to exert pull in the same direction, the rise will be extreme (twelve feet at Boston, not eight). And so will the low. When they line up so as to pull in opposite directions, the tides will *also* be extreme. That brings us to the strange fact that high tide occurs on opposite sides of the globe simultaneously! Who ever would have thought?

The moon and sun are not the sole gravitational forces affecting ocean waters. The earth's gravity comes into play too. It pulls inward towards earth's center, in opposition to the outward pulls of the sun and moon toward their positions of the moment. The inward-pull and the outward-pull occur at differing angles to the molecules of ocean water. These *angles* create a component of the side-pull that is the tide-creating force.

This component acts similarly and simultaneously at directly opposite points on the globe. In conjunction with centrifugal force – force exerted outward on bodies spinning around a joint center of gravity, in this case the sun, earth and moon – it moves particles of water primarily sideways. Let us suppose that the gravitational pull when the moon and sun line up together over the South Atlantic exerts itself on a line through the earth to the floor of, in this instance, the China Sea. The *angle* and *strength* of pull, or *vector* of all gravitational forces nearly equals a similar angle formed on the nearer, South Atlantic side. Thus we have two tides on opposite sides of the globe that rise and fall at the same time in almost equal magnitude. The *vector* of the component forces creates tide; the vectors are nearly the same on opposite sides of the globe at the same instant. (diagram and legend pp. 112-113: **Tide-generating forces**)

The rise and fall of tides in open ocean (about two feet) is almost imperceptible. Only when the sideways-pulled water encounters resistance from underwater topography or immense land barriers does its rise become apparent, being greater or smaller depending on the configurations encountered. Thus the Bay of Fundy's fifty-foot rise and the free-standing Caribbean Islands' small, almost unnoticeable rise.

Tides exist on lakes and inland seas too. The same forces are at work. But given the minuteness of the changes created relative to the size of the body of water, only large oceans sloshing against gigantic land masses produce the most dramatic effects.

Much more can be studied about this subject. Even the basic answers about this seemingly elemental phenomenon are not commonly understood in this, the atomic and space age. We have neglected the study of the oceans until quite recently.

Clearly the tide holds very little practical interest for the lake sailor. For ocean sailors – and lake sailors who sooner or later will find ocean water under their boats – it is a factor to reckon with. It creates mile-wide sand flats on the north-side shore of Cape Cod. It shoals West Bay to a one-inch depth where six hours before we sailed in three or four feet of water (the typical range on Cape Cod's south shore). It creates tidal currents to be planned for and used by cruising sailors. It swings heavy boats at anchor until they foul less affected lighter boats. It influences race outcomes, wave heights, and for all we know the psychological equilibrium of sailors.

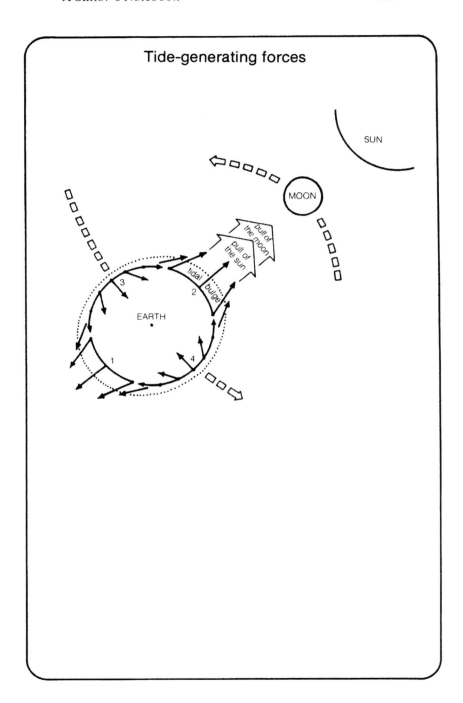

Tide-generating forces

Tide-Generating Forces

Arrows (p. 112) show various directions and magnitude (proportional to length of arrow) of forces generating tides. The forces involved are the pull of the moon's gravity, the pull of the sun's gravity, the pull of the earth's gravity (toward its center) and the centrifugal force of rotation. Differences in the balance among these forces acting on given particles of water at various points on earth create the tide.

Note: The *vector* of the pull of the moon's and sun's gravity and of the centrifugal force of the earth's rotation (around the joint center of gravity of all three bodies) is *nearly the same* on opposite sides of the earth. That causes high tides to occur simultaneously at points 1 and 2, and correspondingly low tides at points 3 and 4.

For inshore ocean sailors, knowing the tide's state is important. Elaborate tables show highs and lows for almost every coastal location in the United States. The tables also show the spread between high and low for each successive tide. In calm conditions the predicted spread will hold. If a powerful wind blows offshore during a receding tide, or vice versa, that tide may well exceed its expected range. An important storm occurring near the time of high tide and having strong onshore winds will add to the tide's height. If a low pressure center passes at the time of a peak-range flood tide, the resultant high water and wave-pounding may produce a coastal disaster.

Keep your copy of the tide tables handy, but also watch for natural signs of the tide. It tilts buoys over in varying degrees; observing this will tell you something about its direction and strength that day. The dark mark left on wet sand as the tide recedes offers a sort of tidal hourglass. So do the watermarks on dock pilings. Where tidal current sluices around objects, it indicates its direction and velocity by ripples in the water. Flotsam and jetsam, sometimes the surface of the water itself, reveal tidal current to the alert eye.

If you know where it is going, you can use the tidal current. An afternoon's pleasure sail works out well if you lay a course that brings you home with the tidal current. Keep in mind that waves will not be as steep when wind and current travel in the same direction, and you'll have a smoother sail. Lay your boat up on the beach at high tide for a free maintenance haulout. Calculate the rise, and use it to sail in otherwise unnavigable water. Calculate the fall, and avoid temporarily dangerous grounds.

The mention of ground brings up the subject of going

aground. In shoal, sandy areas such as West Bay a sailor may develop a practiced style of running aground if he is venturesome and new to the area. One way to handle the embarrassment is to stand up, remove excess clothing – a nattily-dressed visiting English lord sailing with a Cotuit family in the '20s got up and took his clothing off, folded it neatly and placing it on deck, without further comment jumped in naked to help shove off – and jump in as if having stopped for a planned lunch-swim. While in the water, perhaps munching a sandwich, nonchalantly push the boat off. The nonchalance will mark your sailing experience and also help keep your temper down, improving health and life expectancy. Do not forget to push the boat in the direction opposite to the way it went aground. Leave the making of new underwater trenches to the dredging crews.

Of course in bigger boats, bigger problems. Powerful tows may be needed. Or kedging with anchors, rocking, heeling the boat with halyards, boom-weights, anchoring and waiting for the tide to come back in – whatever it takes to get her off. Sadly, when a boat goes up on a rocky shore or reef, she may be finished. It depends on the damage at impact, and/or the damage from wave action lifting the boat up and smashing it down before she can be freed.

The tide may play a well-hidden part in causing big-boat groundings. Its currents have set navigators far off course when closing a continental coast. In fog, lacking electronic navigational aids, the sailor closing a coastline can be headed for unsuspected trouble, having picked up a red number 6 buoy that is fifty miles from the identically marked buoy he thinks he has sighted. Such are the vagaries of our repetitive coastal buoy marking system. Behind the wrong red number 6 may lie rocks rather than the safe harbor expected.

Keep your eye on the tide. It waits for no man, as we know. But rightly caught, it works for all.

·20·

The Other Side of the Cape

•

I have often referred to the Nantucket Sound, or the south side of
Cape Cod, but seldom to its "other" side. Which side is the
"other" depends of course on where the speaker's loyalties
reside. In either case it seems a good idea to pay a visit to the
Cape Cod Bay shore, which stretches from the Cape Cod Canal
to Provincetown. It offers a different world to the sailor.

The Cape juts out into the Atlantic in the familiar shape

of an extended arm bent at the elbow. What would correspond to the biceps and inner forearm – each representing about 30 miles of coastline – meet at right angles, enclosing two sides of Cape Cod Bay. The bay ranges from 30 to 150 feet deep, almost without shoal or obstruction. It is bordered on the western side above the canal by the Plymouth shoreline, which extends 35 miles northward to Minot's Ledge at the beginning of Boston Harbor. The northern end of the bay opens into Massachusetts Bay and the Gulf of Maine.

A perfect place to sail, at first look. It has no hazards like the shoals and islands that ring Nantucket Sound. Here is open, deep water, over nine hundred square miles of it, protected from ocean swells. Yet, in fact, fewer sailboats are seen here than in Nantucket Sound or virtually any other North American body of water so suitably located.

This is all the more remarkable because many of the original Cape Cod seafaring men came from the inside shore. Starting in the 1790s, towns like Dennis, Brewster, Barnstable and Sandwich sent sea captains to Boston and New York in greater numbers than any other section of the country. When the sailing ship era died in the late 1800s, Route 6A through these towns was well dotted with spacious captains' houses complete with "widows' walks." Into them the great captains retired one by one to look out over the bay, live out their days, and often start new enterprises. The towns their riches helped build were picturesque, quiet, and tree-lined and are to this day uniquely charming.

When summer resort development came to the Cape, it grew fastest not here but on the south shore, where land was less expensive, beaches as good, and the water warmer and deep enough for recreational sailors in numerous harbors. By 1930 one found on the bay side only a few small sailboats at Provincetown and Wellfleet, a few at Dennis and Barnstable, a small fleet at a camp in Brewster. Not until crossing to the mainland at Plymouth, Duxbury, and Cohasset did one find significant numbers. Why was – why is – this pleasant bay so thinly populated by sailors?

Certainly not because of a lack of breezes. In summer, winds rotating around the big high lingering near Bermuda, abetted by thermals drawn by the land masses of New England and the Canadian Maritime Provinces, create a strong southwester that blows easily over the low-lying Cape, as described in chapter eighteen. The breeze drops to water level within a few yards of the bay shoreline, blowing at a merry clip. Only six-inch to one-foot waves are encountered as far as a half mile from the north-facing shore even in a spanking twenty-knot breeze. Sailing is ideal in the combined circumstance of strong breeze and smooth water. Strong onshore northerlies – rare in summer – make waves, but these are the only winds that do, and wave heights do not usually exceed three feet. Along the inside shore at Provincetown or Wellfleet the opposite holds; the northerlies and easterlies produce flat water, the southwesterlies bring waves.

The problem with offshore breeezes, as we have noted, is that inexperienced sailors can be lulled into going out too far. Whether this has actually happened often enough to frighten away small-boat sailors from Cape Cod Bay, I do not know. I suspect an instinctive caution is struck in almost every adult upon encountering this combination of conditions. But you cannot count on it, especially not in younger people. I know of two canoeists who, during the years I sailed at a camp along this coastline, went too far offshore. They could not paddle back against increasing waves and wind. They were teenagers, young women from another camp three miles up the shore. A rescue failed when their camp outboard was unable to sight the canoe, probably by then overturned in the choppy, white-capped water. When a Coast Guard Duck arrived some two hours later, it too could not find the canoe. It was found two days later on the Wellfleet shore, ten miles across the bay. The bodies of the young women were washed ashore several days after that on the banks of Namskaket Creek, four miles down the beach from their starting point. The camp closed within a week, never to reopen.

More recently two lives were lost in a similar way. According to a report in the *Cape Cod Times* on August 22, 1980, two people set out from the North Truro beach near Wellfleet in a boardboat with the wind at twenty-five knots from the northeast – directly offshore from the Truro beach. The young man, twenty-three, and woman, twenty-one, were seen from the beach to tip over and recover twice. They capsized a third time, but no one could be seen climbing back aboard. A rescue boat put out from the beach. Forty minutes later the boardboat was picked up by a fishing boat three miles offshore – that is how fast these boardboats will blow away from you in a high wind. No one was on or near the boat. One floating life jacket was found.

Sailing is inhibited along the bay's shore by tidal flats. Someone who has not seen the flats cannot guess at the size of the problem. At low tide the sandy plains extend nearly a mile offshore in places. If your boat is moored along this shoreline, it may stand high and dry for half the day. Tides here rise and fall eight to twelve feet, as at Boston. The flats are caused by the extremely gradual incline of the bay's floor. Bare feet are delightfully tickled on the little ridges left in the sand by receding waves, and being able to walk to your boat is certainly convenient. But what do you do when you get there and find it sitting in a sea of sand?

One solution is to use inner and outer moorings. The outer is placed so far out the boat is in a couple of feet of water even at low tide. The inner is placed at half the distance to shore. You must plan where to moor when coming in from a sail, depending on the predicted tide when you next intend to sail. If the tide crosses you up, your boat will either be hopelessly aground at the inner mooring, or perhaps a mile's dinghy ride away at the outer. This stimulates careful study of the tide tables. It also develops the habit of planning ahead.

Despite encouraging these laudable disciplines, the flats have probably dampened small-boat activity along the inside shore more than any factor. Few harbors here have channels that are usable at all tides for small boats, so few that they accommodate a relatively tiny boat population. Some harbors that had deep water in the nineteenth century have shoaled since. Only Provincetown and Sandwich (at a marina inside the canal) now have sizable "deep"-water harbors. Barnstable and Wellfleet have dredged channels into moderately sized boat basins, as have Sesuit and Rock Harbor on a smaller scale. Thus, in about sixty miles of coastline from Cape Cod Canal to Provincetown, there are only six small harbors – not much to work with. No wonder we see fewer sailboats here than on the south shore, which has literally three times as many suitable harbors in a much shorter stretch.

I remember how I came to a sailing camp here at age seven. I had begun to sail the preceding summer. My family had rented a cottage on the south side of the Cape at Lewis Bay, part of Hyannis harbor. Hyannis had an active fleet of Cape Cod Knockabouts – pert, pretty 18-foot sloops that had a reputation for speed and ability in the summer sou'westers. I loved to watch them race. I had my favorite and remember the name: *Blueboy,* which under the talented Gardner Schirmer won most of the races.

Early that summer my appendix kicked up and was removed. During the recuperation period my mother – who worked all day managing a new business branch my father had established in Hyannis – hired an extra baby sitter to see that I recovered properly. By good luck she found Thayer, a young man whose family lived nearby and owned a Knockabout. He promptly put me in his boat. I was in heaven. He took me sailing every day for weeks knowing that it kept me content and quiet. All the while he got paid for doing something he liked. Heaven all around.

One day toward the middle of August he showed up at the dock with a pretty girl in tow. I was tickled at the prospect of this exciting addition to our outings and leapt for the boat. But my mentor, who was about eighteen, for the first time insisted I wear a lifejacket. For some reason – I'm not sure why really; something to do with the suspect cause of the change, I suppose – I refused. He persisted. I said it was unfair, after all this time, etc.

"Put it on," he demanded, holding out the bulky, ugly kapok-filled jacket.

"No, I won't."

"Put it on or you won't ever sail on this boat again, starting today."

"No. *She* isn't wearing one!"

"Okay, you're off the boat."

I smiled. I didn't think he meant it. How could he end the great times we'd had?

But Thayer and the young lady jumped into the lovely white-hulled Knockabout – its name was *Wee Skewer,* I think – and sailed away. I never got on that boat again. Thayer resigned as my baby sitter and was seen many an afternoon sailing on Lewis Bay with the pretty girl close by his side.

I was angry and hurt, and puzzled by my own self-defeating stubbornness. So I was very excited the next summer to arrive at Camp Monomoy on the *other* side of the Cape and see a whole fleet of sailboats waiting on their moorings. They didn't have to wait long. Never mind that half of them were sitting on the flats at low tide – and the others half a mile out in shallow water. The camp's double mooring system worked quite well. I spent ten happy summers as camper and counselor at that camp – most of it sailing!

The Cape has a third and a fourth side as well. The third lies along the Buzzards Bay shore on the outside of the Cape's shoulder, if you follow the bent-arm analogy. This coast is dotted with harbors from Woods Hole to the west end of the canal. They are filled with sailboats, contributing to the many seen on Buzzards Bay on almost any summer day. The harbors are small, indented between rocky fingers of land a little harsher than the sand-fringed boundaries of the Cape's other coasts. They have names like Quisset, West Falmouth, Megansett, Pocasset and Phinneys. Many Cape Cod Knockabouts, Beetlecats, Bullseyes, Sunfish and cruising auxiliaries are found here, and some avid sailors. They have to be avid, for they face the tooth-rattling Buzzards Bay chop when a strong southwest wind funnels up the bay against an ebbing tide, as it often does.

The fourth side is the Outer Beach, forty miles of almost

unbroken white sand from Chatham to Provincetown made famous in the writings of Wyman Richardson *(The House on Nauset Marsh),* Henry David Thoreau *(Cape Cod)* and Henry Beston *(The Outermost House).*   This is a land of crashing Atlantic surf, of high dunes and uplands precipitously hanging cliff-like over the wide beach, of sand nearly too hot to walk on in summer, washed by water almost too cold to swim in. Not a single deep harbor is found along the Outer Beach. The only break in the beach is at Nauset Inlet, which will take a knowledgeable local boatman in a shallow-draft boat safely into Orleans town cove. [The great northeast storm of 1992 cut a new inlet that allows direct access to Chatham Harbor from the Atlantic – also used only by boatmen with precise local knowledge.] It's a shore for sailors to avoid, for all boats to shun. Exposed to prevailing easterly storms, without shelter, plagued by slanting onshore currents, pounded by waves that roll across a 2500-mile fetch from Europe, this beach has claimed the bones of many a ship and sailor. In Beston's day, the nearest neighbor to his outermost house was a Coast Guard lifeboat station at Nauset. From there an all-night foot patrol walked the beach in search of shipwreck and disaster. The Coast Guard station still stands, though foot patrols no longer pace the night. The dangers have not changed, and despite loran and radar, modern freighters still go up on this shore.

Recently I heard a radio news broadcast of the recovery off Highland Light (a station further up the beach) of the leg bone of a fisherman lost last winter. His boat had failed to return to Provincetown. The bone, with a telltale fracture matching that of the missing man, was brought up from two-hundred-foot depth by another fishing boat's net. For one of these thirty- or forty-foot vessels to be fishing off the Outer Beach in the month of February is an act of courage if not downright foolhardiness. The temporary fall and winter mild spells can suddenly turn into fierce storms. On a hot July day, looking from atop the highlands over the Outer Beach at the small figures of sunbathers some one hundred feet below on the sand, and gazing at the wondrously blue Atlantic stretching away to the horizon, one sees a scene of dazzling beauty. The tranquility of the moment belies the powerful forces at rest. This shoreline is not for recreational sailors. The few who sail along it in summer must pick the day carefully. It is not a place to be caught when the storm winds blow.

Cape Cod Bay, however, someday may support more sailing activity. It awaits extensive harbor development along the inside shore from Sandwich to Provincetown and a better solution to the inner-outer mooring dilemma. If either happens, the broad and protected bay waters should become a sailor's mecca. The bay would make an ideal site for racing, especially for a class requiring fifteen- or twenty-mile course legs. A natural bowl, surrounded on three sides by land, largely unaffected by currents or ocean waves, full of breeze – what a grand amphitheater it would make for the America's Cup competition. By using particular course layouts, spectators on land could see both the starting and windward marks.

Perhaps this will occur someday, with a TV satellite hookup, a consortium of beer and gear sponsors and the New England Patriots cheerleaders to collect tickets at the bridges!

·21·

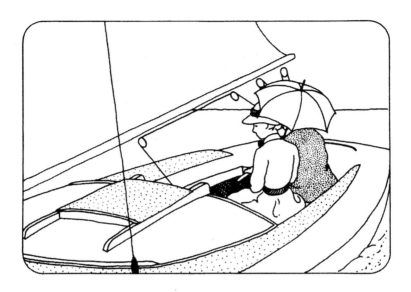

One Small Boat:
A Passage through Time

•

Our boat was built in the winter of 1913-14 and launched in the spring. Eighty-seven years later, as I write, she is still actively sailed and sometimes raced. Lord knows how long, with proper care, a wooden boat may go on.

How she came to her long life, who owned her, what adventures she took part in – these questions naturally have come to mind. Over the years friends and acquaintances have volunteered information. But the story remained tantalizingly incomplete for a long time. I resolved to trace the tale of this one small boat.

With the help of many people, not least Jamie Hess, who has traced the histories of my boat's entire class, the pieces finally fell into place. Hess's painstaking research in the early 1970s of the recent lineage of every Senior built was published in 1976. It listed the then owner of each accurately numbered Senior. I am much indebted to him.

The Wianno Senior class has been successful. The Crosbys conceived and built them along the lines of the best gaff-rigged racing boats of the time, and they have outlasted many. Our boat is far from alone in her antiquity. Of the 14 boats built the first winter, 1 still sails today. Of the 160 built of wood between 1914 and 1976, only 15 are known wrecked, lost, burned or abandoned. Most of the remaining 145 wooden boats are still sailing. Since 1986, thirty-five Seniors have been built with Fiberglas hulls, trimmed and sparred by Crosbys handsomely in traditional wood. About 40 boats race, including most of the new 'glas boats. One built in 1930, the great class champion and benefactor Dave Steere's *Venture* (85), was grandly sailed to victory in the last tough race of the 1979 regatta season by her owner, who was quite possibly more than a decade older than his boat. *Venture* may now be seen, smartly restored, at the Osterville Historical Society's Marine Museum.

In the great fire of 2003 at Crosbys, twenty-one Seniors were destroyed. All but three were wooden boats – the cream of the racing crop. Since then almost all the top racers have built beautiful new 'glas boats.

This remarkable longevity in years and numbers testifies to the integrity in design and construction of the boats. And obviously their owners have loved and cared for them well. One

Senior – the late Jim Hinkle's *Fantasy* (11) – is in inventory at the Mystic Seaport Museum, part of a display of notable small sailing craft. Another – John F. Kennedy's blue-hulled *Victura* (94), beautifully rebuilt and refinished – points seaward on her tilted pedestal in front of the Kennedy Library at the edge of Boston Harbor, a haunting riderless steed stopped in full stride. And *Tirza* (7) now resides in the in-the-water exhibit of notable sailing craft at the Museum of Yachting, Newport, R.I.

Other good classes from the early times have survived – the Herreshoff S-boats and Bullseyes; the Stars; the big Idem gaffers of 1898 in upper New York state – but none more impressively than the Seniors with regard to the proportion of the original boats still sailing over a like span of years. So the fact that ours, number 7, survives is not so much remarkable as it is typical and illustrative.

The boat's first owner was apparently Jack Tiernan of Osterville, Massachusetts and Cairo, Illinois. I must say *apparently* because the first written record I have found connecting Jack Tiernan to the boat's ownership goes back to 1915 rather than 1914. This leaves the possibility that someone else owned her during the first year. The late, beloved Max Crosby, who helped build all the first boats while in his teens and whose fairness and skill played a vital part in the construction of nearly every Senior thereafter, told me in the mid-1970s that he thought there might have been an owner before Jack Tiernan. But the name always escaped Uncle Max and no one else remembered until Merrill (Deak) Crosby, another of the talented Crosby boat builders, came up with the name Franklin Robinson in a conversation with Anne P. Halliday. Anne's friendship and talent for unearthing good information greatly helped my hunt for the boat's history.

Mr. Robinson was in 1914 a professor of music at the Juilliard School in New York, a conductor of note. By coincidence he summered in a house overlooking West Bay owned subsequently by Anne Halliday's family from Cairo and Memphis, Tennessee as a vacation home. She retained and lived on a rear section of the property bordering Aunt Tempy's Pond almost until her death in 1998, at the age of 98.

The cost of a new Senior in 1914 was $650. A letter from Jack Tiernan's cousin and sometime crew gives a little of the history and flavor of those times:

Mount Dora, Florida
April 29th, 1974

Dear Mr. Ulian –

I do thank you for your very interesting letter concerning the history of #7 Crosby cat. [Strictly speaking the Senior is not a catboat as it carries three sails – main, jib and spinnaker – while a cat normally carries one, a large main, on a mast placed far forward in the very eyes of the bow.] As Ann has probably told you our family travelled from Cairo, Illinois to Osterville, first by train, then by car. We spent our first years at East Bay Lodge and my memory recalls 1915. I was 13 years old. My cousin John Craig Aisthorpe was 11 – we were then crew in #7 operated by Cousin Jack Tiernan.

My last summer with Cousin Jack was the summer of 1924. 1925 I spent in Europe. We returned to the Cape in 1926. Father rented Ralph Crosby's house. 1927 and 1928 I visited with Ann's grandmother in her house on East Bay and still remember #7 and Cousin Jack. Then 1929 with two friends we stayed at the Crosby House for golf and I do not remember sailing with Cousin Jack nor with Ann.

Then the stock break and I was in the brokerage business in Chicago. So I did not see the Cape again until 1935.

Those were wonderful years and wish my memory was more complete and exact.

[Signed]
Russell Halliday

The *Ann* mentioned in the letter is Anne Pillow Halliday, an Osterville summer resident in the early 1900's, a vigorous year-round resident and sailor at the age of eighty, and in those days the owner-skipper of Wianno Senior #4, *A. P. H.*

Jack Tiernan named his boat *Patsy.* The notebooks of the Wianno Yacht Club list *Patsy* in the racing results for the years 1917-1922 under her original sail number, 7, skippered by "J. Tiernan." From about 1923-1929 the notebooks list her still as *Patsy,* now carrying sail number 29, J. Tiernan skipper. In those years, when you bought a new sail, you got a new number with it.

Jack Tiernan had fallen in love as a boy with the beauty of the Great Lakes schooners of the day. According to Anne Halliday he kept *Patsy* neat and pretty, flaking down lines with a precision good schooner crews might have envied. He took pleasure in his boat, sailing often, fussing over it much. I am glad of that because according to the notebooks he did not do too well at the races, even after buying his new sail.

In 1929 or 1930, whether because of the market crash or for other reasons, Jack Tiernan sold his boat to the Morris Ernst family of Nantucket and New York City. By the time I called Mr. Ernst in the spring of 1974, the renowned lawyer (he won the admission of James Joyce's *Ulysses* to this country, among other famous censorship and civil-liberties victories) had forgotten the details of the family's ownership of *Patsy*. But he was interested in her history. "You ought to write a biography of the boat for one of the sailing magazines," he said. He asked me to send him a brief letter relating "just the facts found so far." I promised to do my best. In 1976 I finally did write him the facts I had uncovered. Mr. Ernst's secretary replied. He had died that spring.

Later, Morris Ernst's son Roger kindly furnished some of his memories of the boat. Roger Ernst must have been very young at the time, but he recalled *Patsy* fondly. The family kept her moored in Nantucket harbor in front of their house and sailed her often and with pleasure. He graciously asked us to sail over and revisit her old home, which we did in 1984.

Roger Ernst could not recall exactly when the family sold *Patsy*. But her next owners did. Young Carl Barus of Bass River and Upper Montclair, New Jersey, bought her in 1938 with most of his life's savings. Mrs. Jane Barus, his mother and a great lady, tells the story of how it happened and how *Patsy's* name came to be changed:

Upper Montclair, N. J.
September 11, 1975

Dear Dick –

I promised to write you the story about the original
name of Carl's boat – so here it is. When he was a
baby we started a little savings account for him, and
by the summer of 1938 it amounted to (I believe)
$800.00. By this time he had followed in the family
tradition and had become an excellent sailor –
having been coached by his father, who was also
very good at the helm. So he bought the Senior
Wianno then named *Patsy*. I believe it took all of his
savings account. He had that spring taken what was
known as the Johnson-O'Connor aptitude tests at
Stevens Institute and had found (to his own surprise
I think) that he had a good musical ear and memory.
The opera *Die Valkyrie* appealed to him at the time –
and so the brass *Patsy* letters were removed and the
boat was named *Valkyrie*. Carl practically lived on
her in the summer – and took many long cruises. But
my husband, who was a hoarder of everything that
could possibly – however improbably – come in
useful, kept the old letters. Carl graduated from
Brown and enlisted in the Navy, and we took over
the boat for him. He was in the Pacific for four
years, and then became a radar instructor for naval
officers in this country until after the war was over.
From that time on he did not have the leisure to care
for the boat himself. And at some point – I can't
remember just when – his father and I decided we
had had enough of racing – having been at it since
our teens – and we sold the *Valkyrie,* as you know,
and bought a Junior Wianno – which was the only
one on the river – and hence couldn't be raced. As I

remember it, she had no name at the time and there was much family discussion about what to call her. We had formerly had a Cape Cod Knockabout called *Sea Pup,* so we thought of *Sea Dog* etc. etc. But Peter Barus – Carl's second son – came up with SALTY! This *delighted* his grandfather, who forthwith produced the PATSY letters. So we used the S, A, T, and Y – and bought a brass L! No doubt the P is still lurking around somewhere.

Incidentally, 1938 was the year of the first hurricane to hit the Cape in 100 years. Carl and I took the *Valkyrie* out and proved that you can lay a Wianno down flat and bring her up again. It was quite a sail.

Sorry this is such a messy scrawl. I'm getting to be a shaky old crone – and my hand isn't steady.

The best of luck to you and the Wianno #7.

Sincerely –

Jane Barus

P. S. Correction –

Carl says the boat cost only $650. He bought her the summer before his Sophomore year at Brown.

The Barus family sailed the boat until 1953. The years saw a cruise to Maine undertaken by Carl Barus with two friends, and many races at Bass River in which *Valkyrie* was successful against others of her class, apparently with Carl's skillful father Max often at her tiller. The boat was moored in the river opposite the Barus home. She has in recent years gone back to lie at their dock during the biannual Bass River regatta. Some of the present members of the Barus family still enjoy going for a sail on her at regatta time, and are very welcome, too.

On August 5, 1953, *Valkyrie* was sold to Robert L. Small of West Dennis, Massachusetts:

> August 5, 1953
>
> In consideration of the sum of Five Hundred Dollars ($500.00) and the payment by the purchaser of one half of the broker's $50.00 commission, receipt whereof is hereby acknowledged, I hereby sell my Wianno Senior Knock-about [a generic term for a two-sailed small boat; also the name of a popular class of marconi-rigged Cape Cod 18-footers mentioned in Chapter 20], "Valkyrie", together with her sails, equipment, and mooring, to Robert L. Small, of West Dennis, Cape Cod, Massachusetts, all as now located at Ship Shops Inc., Bass River, Cape Cod, Massachusetts, together with any and all her sails, if any, that may be elsewhere in my possession. I certify that the boat is free and clear of all debts and other encumbrances, and that her storage is paid up in full to date of sale. I am making no other warranties as to the condition of the property sold.
>
> Maxwell Barus

Bob Small is the son of the late Joe Small, a well-known Cape Cod sailor who had been commodore of the Bass River Yacht Club and a president of the Southern Massachusetts Yacht Racing Association. The Commodore Joseph E. Small Memorial

Trophy, competed for by southern Massachusetts sailors, is today the single-handed championship trophy of the district.

Bob Small now lives in Huntington, Long Island. He has told me that when he put the boat in the water, she had been laid up for three years. She had big spaces between all her planks, as much as one-inch spaces between the gaps in the oak planking of her deadwood. Her paint was hanging "like moss." She sunk for one month after being put in, then pulled together beautifully. Next year he had her refastened and she was tight. She went fast, Bob Small recalls, particularly upwind, pointing exceptionally well. She won a number of trophies. But she was slow downwind – they lost several races that way. While he owned the Senior, Bob Small helped originate the present Bass River regatta.

The mast was in awful shape, rotted and weak, Bob recalls. It snapped one breezy day off Bass River when the boat hit a wave and stopped dead and the mast kept going. Bob Small got her a new mast and new sails, reverting for the first time since Jack Tiernan's early days to the number 7. He had her wooded down inside and out and added a cove stripe, gold-leafed. She looked beautiful.

In 1957 at Edgartown the boat had a serious accident. At the regatta a thirty-footer came up under 7, which was on starboard tack, and plowed into the boat's middle, breaking the oak coaming, toe rail, boom and sail track, and twisting the centerboard. A girl was thrown out of the boat on impact. Joe Small was at 7's tiller, and son Bob was worried for his safety because the larger boat came right back aboard after the first impact. The Senior righted herself, however, and the other boat rode up so high it went directly above Commodore Small's head without touching him. No one was hurt. The repair bill was

$421, Bob remembers (about $8,400 at boatyard labor rates today – about $100/hour, vs. $3/hour then). The boat did not leak afterwards.

When he started work on his Ph.D., Bob Small found he had sailed the Senior three times in two summers. So on October 3, 1959, he sold her to Arthur W. Frostholm for $1550.

The Frostholm family lived in West Yarmouth year-round. Arthur Frostholm recalls that he sailed the boat for one season, the summer of 1960, during which the family had fun with it. The following winter she stayed outside in his backyard – probably her first winter outdoors in thirty-six years. Her next owners, James P. Ryan and his wife Peg, bought her from Frostholm on February 19, 1961.

Peg Ryan remembers the date well, because on that evening the Ryans celebrated their engagement with dinner at Eugene's, a restaurant in Middleboro halfway between Boston and Cape Cod. Given its double significance, the dinner was a great success. On April 17, 1961, the Ryans sailed 7 from Cape Cod to Continental Marina, Quincy, near their home in Jamaica Plain outside of Boston. She was solid and tight; no trace of a leak. They sailed her all that summer and the next in Quincy Bay and Boston harbor. But in 1963 when they launched her, she would not stop leaking.

First Jim Ryan, who had done his own maintenance work, and then the people at Continental Marina tried to stop the leaking, which was caused by rot around the centerboard box. Nothing worked. The boat would not float. The Ryans by now were in love with their Senior. They had just bought a pretty green and white spinnaker. On St. Patrick's Day 1963 or soon after, they looked forward to cutting a fine figure sailing in the harbor. Not yet prepared to give up their dream, they loaded the boat on a flatbed trailer and at some expense had her brought to the Crosby yard for repair.

Theirs had been a long engagement. Three weeks before the wedding date, the Crosbys informed Jim Ryan of the probable cost of repairs. It left him with a difficult decision concerning the allocation of his resources. Jim Ryan's wife says he still jokes that he made the wrong choice the day he traded the Senior to Doug Higham, a boat carpenter at Crosbys. He got in return a sound little Bigelow catboat, which Peg remembers as eighteen feet long and cute, and he conserved enough money to launch their marriage successfully. They keep the green and white spinnaker in their basement. It has never been out of the bag.

Doug Higham was – and is – an experienced boat-builder. He put the Senior in the yard at his house in Osterville and went to work. With the help and advice of his two sons, Bill Crosby Jr. and other friends and boatyard workers who dropped by from time to time, he performed a major rebuild and a minor miracle. The keel was removed, as were the garboards, the sheer planks, the cockpit sole and bulkheads and the entire deck and cuddy cabin. Then all these parts were built again new, using the original patterns.

The centerboard box was thought to be too far gone to replace or rebuild without opening up the possibility of future loss of the boat. Higham therefore removed the box and plugged the opening in the keelson. He built a new centerboard to fit the remaining slot in the keel and deadwood. It had the same doweled oak construction and length as a normal Senior board but only about one-third the lateral plane. This is what Jamie Hess has called a half-centerboard. Number 7 is the only boat in the fleet so rebuilt. [Since the earlier versions of this book more than one Senior has been similarly rebuilt. At least thirteen of the older ones now have no centerboards at all, their keelson slots having been plugged to avoid chronic leakage. Nowadays, using modern epoxy glues, the box can be rebuilt tightly – at considerable expense. The guts of the boat must be removed and reinstalled new.]

Higham felt pleased with his work, having with one stroke eliminated the large box that took up so much space inside the cuddy and the cockpit and is always subject to leaking, and made the boat tight again.

In the spring of 1964 she was launched, freshly painted, gleaming white. As a cruising sailor who almost never raced Higham rigged her to cruise, paying no mind to racing gear or tune. In fact in his opinion the boat would not be competitive. He particularly anticipated a problem in staying with the fleet upwind with the new half-centerboard.

Over the years we have brought her up, little by little, to something nearer racing tune. As for winning, she has recently begun to win some junior-skipper races against other good Seniors, with Steve at the tiller and his peers as crew. In time, as he and his crews gain more experience, she might again give a creditable account of herself against adult skippers. [She did. Steve won the 1982 July series in her, among other victories.]

In July of 1964 I first saw 7 at Crosbys and sailed her. I determined to buy her then. I have related how I finally succeeded in doing so. But not before Giles Wanamaker, formerly of Greenwich, CT and just moved down Cape to Orleans, saw her sitting prettily at Crosby's with the name *Valkyrie* on her transom. The very same name as that of his former yacht. He inquired how much. Doug Higham figured he was entitled to X number of dollars per hour for his labors. He estimated a thousand skilled hours had gone into the rebuild. He did the multiplication. Giles Wanamaker wrote a check for the product on the spot.

In the spring of 1965, Wanamaker and Sid Swan, his Orleans insurance man, sailed 7 eastward to Stage Harbor, Chatham. They hitched a tow into Chatham Harbor through the slim channel behind Morris Island [impossible to do since alterations to the harbor by the great northeast storm of 1992, the so-called "Perfect Storm."]. They sailed her up Pleasant Bay. She was moored in the hidden pond where I found her three years later as told in chapter twelve.

Giles Wanamaker lavished attention on the boat. The cove stripe of Bob Small's day was again leafed with gold. A gold-leafed quarterboard went on her transom, the name carved by Doug Higham himself. Many coats of varnish were carefully laid on her brightwork by a Norwegian working for the Arey's Pond boatyard. He had a special touch with a brush. Every aspect of her care was lovingly done.

In late June, 1967, I purchased the boat from Giles Wanamaker. I received the following document:

Orleans, Mass.

June 30, 1967

Received from Richard Ulian the sum of one dollar and other valuable considerations, in payment in full for one Wianno Senior, hull number 7, named "Valkyrie."

[Signed]
Giles A. Wanamaker

I sailed her around Monomoy Point through Pollack Rip

into Nantucket Sound. ("You're going over Chatham Bars and through the rip in *that?*" one grizzled old fisherman said to me while we waited for the fog to lift, eyeing the relatively small sailboat moored off the fish dock at Chatham. He didn't know what a Senior can do. The day I chose was calm and the trip uneventful, if a little scary.) I arrived in Osterville on July 4, 1967. She sailed from Osterville for fourteen summers and from Cotuit since 1982, attended to and maintained by one or the other Crosby yards and increasingly by me, with the help of Deborah and sons Mark and Steve. She remained perfectly tight for ten or eleven years. She has started to weep at the garboards rather more than we like now, but she is getting attention, and we find a bit of caulking usually solves the problem.

Although she raced semi-regularly with the rest of the fleet for most of the years in Osterville, she is a family boat, not strictly a racing vehicle. We use her for pleasure sailing, for giving lessons, for whatever comes along, and like all the Seniors, she responds handsomely.

Her name is new. When I first saw *Valkyrie* on her transom I was not as entranced as Giles Wanamaker. Collector of slain German heroes from the battlefield was not the role I had in mind for the boat, Valhalla not my choice of a cruising destination.

I resolved to change it, though three years earlier Doug Higham had warned me not to, recounting the boatman's ancient tale of bad luck accompanying a name change. I believe he thought *Valkyrie* was her original name. None of us knew then about *Patsy.* I checked with Teddy Crosby at Crosby's. "Put any name you want on it," he said. "It's your boat. Just do it while she's on dry land and the change won't bring bad luck."

During that summer I searched the Osterville Library for

a suitable name. There I found the story of a certain Miss Lovell of the village. In 1818, it seems, she married Andrew Crosby, one of the early members of the famous boat-building family. Late in life, the story goes, Andrew Crosby drew the plans for a new kind of Crosby boat. Sometime along the way he and his wife had joined the Spiritualism movement, popular at the time. The members believed the living could communicate with the spirits of the dead. Mrs. Crosby became a medium, able it was said to make this connection. Andrew died before his new boat could be built. His two sons, Horace and Worthington, undertook building the boat to prove the design's ability. When they encountered a difficult problem in construction, legend says, Mrs. Crosby held a séance in order to get further instructions from Andrew.

The boat was launched in 1850 and was a great success. She sailed faster than previous boats "thrice for one," we are told, and came about "quick as a cat," giving origin to the designation of the many boats the Crosbys built subsequently that followed her design principles: catboats. It marked a turning point in their business.

In the prevailing biblical fashion of those Cape Cod days, Mrs. Andrew Crosby's given name was Tirzah. During the spring of 1968, while number 7 was most assuredly on dry land, Teddy Crosby, Tirzah's great-great-grandson, carved the letters T I R Z A on our boat's transom. They were then gold-leafed. Number 7 had her new name.

It doubly pleased me. In the late 1940s I had made several trips to the Middle East. A revival of biblical Hebrew had occurred in Israel. I recalled in particular a young woman named Tirza. (The current Israeli-English spelling drops the *h*.) She was the highly respected leader of a small kibbutz at the foot of

Mount Tabor where I lived for some time and encountered great hospitality. I admired her determination and good sense and was happy that she and Mrs. Crosby shared the boat's name.

Later, when we discovered the original name, *Patsy,* it seemed too late to change *Tirza* back. The kids would not hear of it. Now, if people would just pronounce it *Teer-tsa,* the old way, instead of *Ter-za,* which seems to have come down from Cape Cod of the 1800's, I would be completely happy. It means delight.

[This translation is not wholly accurate. The name more literally means *desire* or *wish.* There's some doubt. It's a noun taken probably from the infinitive *leer'-ot* (to want). From *leer'-ot* and its conjugated form *ruh-tsa'* (I, you, etc. *want*) may derive the feminine biblical name *Teer-tsa'* (a desired one). This very educated etymological guess came from the late, famed Dr. Yael Teitz, an old friend and retired professor at Tel Aviv University, and her daughter Ta'al, both Ph.D.'s in the biological sciences, in response to my insistent questioning during their 1991 visit to Cotuit.]

·22·

The Cruise of the Argo
·

Suppose you are an experienced small-boat sailor. You would like to try sailing a large cruising boat but you do not know if you can handle it. Nonetheless, on the strength of your experience in little boats your friends charter a forty-eight-footer from a much too trusting acquaintance of theirs. Autumn has come to New England, a time of tranquil spells broken by sudden fierce storms.

I once sailed a cruising boat under these circumstances. With one exception my friends and crew were inexperienced. The scenes that I recall go something like this.

Marblehead. The puddles in the parking lot reflect a gray, drizzly September sky. A light northeast wind curls ominous fingers of fog around the streetlights. Through the murky dusk I see my crew's car. I lift the duffle out of my own car and start down the ramp. We're here, all right, but can we sail the boat that lies along the dock at the ramp's end?

Argo Navis is a wood ketch, twenty-five tons of boat. My experience is mostly in boats of up to sixteen feet weighing about five hundred pounds. I have sailed thirty footers and a thirty-six footer on widely separated occasions. My crew's limited experience is also in small boats. Dick has done Navy time on shore launches and other powerboats, and some sailing with his dad. The rest of the group's sailing experience consists of two passenger outings in a small boat by Ben and his wife Charlotte; Dick's wife Dede has done about as much; Sandy and Carol are starting fresh.

The weather this foggy first night certainly looks forbidding. I feel anxious. I see Dick and Ben, blurred shadows on the deck. Their welcome is almost enough to calm me.

Dick has already done the boat checkout with the owner, who has left trustingly for a cocktail party. Nice he has such confidence. But I do not know whether to be relieved by this, or concerned about his judgment.

"He said we might have trouble with the throttle," Dick says. "The linkage broke. They wired it temporarily a couple of weeks ago."

Ugh.

"No other problems we know of," Dick said. "The tanks are topped off. I've been over the boat and I think I know where everything is. There won't be any activity at the town dock tonight, the owner says. He thinks we can lie here overnight."

I look the boat over. The *Argo* was strongly built for a circumnavigation thirty years ago. She made it as far as the Galapagos. She had been bought and sold a few times since then. She looks husky but a little tired.

My view of large cruising boats comes chiefly from a few careful readings of the applicable chapters in H. A. Calahan's old-fashioned but thoroughly excellent *Learning to Cruise*. Everything on deck seems to be as Calahan predicted. Other than the boom gallows and varnished wheel, the gear is familiar to a small-boat sailor, but oversized. After a few minutes I start to feel better.

"Want to go below?" Ben asks. "We've got the radio tuned in to the weather. Well, how do you like her?"

"Looks okay. Big, isn't she?"

Ben made a reassuring face. He was the one who got the boat for us through a business connection. His faith in my sailing ability – those two previous outings were with me – had no known limits. He led the way below.

While Charlotte, a caterer on land, served up coffee and doughnuts, the radio broadcast good cheer. A fair and warm day was forecast for tomorrow.

We were cozy and dry in the cabin. Soon we made up the bunks and turned in to sleep.

The boat lay bow towards shore, the stern extending several feet beyond the dock's outer end. We could not pull ahead at low tide as there was insufficient water under the bow. Naturally, at three in the morning when the tide was high a lobsterman thumped on our hull. We sleepily pushed the boat forward to clear the dock for his boat to come in and load traps. He groused quite rightly that we should not tie up at the town dock overnight.

Morning dawned calm and sunny. Sandy and Carol now joined us. After breakfast we cast off and slowly backed out.

Very slowly. Calahan's advice is to proceed as in a small boat – but much more slowly. Very sound advice.

I was surprised at how easily *Argo* handled. Her great bulk glided gently from the dock. The wind was light, which helped my confidence. Under power, we inched carefully around the moored boats crowded in the harbor. Soon we rounded Marblehead Neck. The sun came out. Lobster pot buoys dotted the sparkling channel. Peel sweaters, don bikinis.

We hoisted the sails without trouble. We shut off the engine and under main, mizzen and big genny *Argo* heeled to a gentle northeast breeze, Provincetown bound. This was the life!

The big ketch seemed to move sluggishly, however. Inspection revealed a line dragging from under the transom at an angle that suggested we were pulling something heavy. We hauled the line in, surprisingly hard to do, and found a lobster pot at its end. The line had snagged on our prop, no doubt. We cut it free, not wishing to poach from a lobsterman presumably ready to make the time-honored response with a well-aimed shotgun.

We could not hazard using the engine until the prop was cleared. It seemed unwise to send someone over the side a mile offshore in icy waters. Marblehead – narrow and full of boats – did not invite an attempt to reenter under sail alone. So we left the prop fouled and rolled lazily along, making the fifty or so miles to Race Point in one long tack. It was a lovely day for a first sail. By four o'clock we could see the spire of Provincetown Monument, a matchstick on the horizon. We had seen one boat all day, a commercial fishing trawler.

It took two hours in the dying evening breeze to reach

Wood End and then round Long Point, sheets eased, and head into the harbor. It was blessedly uncrowded. We dropped the genny on the way in. Where the chart showed eight- to ten-foot depths off Provincetown Wharf, the helm went over and *Argo* docilely rounded up in the evening stillness. When she stopped, the anchor was let go and set. No problems from the lack of an engine yet.

We dinghied ashore for dinner. A somnolent postseason Provincetown echoed our footsteps up and down Commercial Street. We returned to the boat early and turned in.

The morning weather forecast called for a partly cloudy day with light northeast winds. But it also stated that small craft warnings might go up after noontime, with heavy squalls possible.

Out first priority was to clear the prop. No one wanted to dive into the fifty-degree water. At that temperature water will fast turn you blue with cold. Dick created a diversion by raising the Race Point Coast Guard station on the radio and asking for a better suggestion. In short order a launch with six or seven Guardsmen appeared. Whether magnetized by our female contingent or simply happy to escape routine for a while, they lay off our port quarter and chatted for half an hour. Their advice, of course, was to jump in and clear the wrapped line. Or haul the boat. The latter idea seemed to amuse them greatly.

Sandy apparently had the wheel when the trap was snagged. Be that as it may, he volunteered. In three brave attempts, clad in a bathing suit, he cut and cleared the line away. He reported the water felt very, very cold.

A window-shopping trip among the half-closed sandal shops quickly exhausted Provincetown's lonely late September charms. Our crew wanted to shove off. Boredom was setting in.

The sky looked leaden. I felt that we might have a rough trip to Cape Cod Canal but agreed to try it if the majority wished. We voted to go. It is not, however, necessarily a good idea to run a boat by majority vote of the crew. That's why ships have captains.

As the *Argo* motored out, sunlight broke through the morning haze. Sails and bikinis were soon the order of the day. The air was cool, the sun warm. The wind was so light that, running dead before it, the boat scarcely moved, so we reached off toward Billingsgate Island, making slow progress.

By noon we had Wellfleet abeam. We jibed directly for the canal, bringing the breeze over the starboard quarter. Carol, the least experienced, took the helm. Everyone settled in for a pleasant afternoon's sail. None of us looked at a dark line of clouds over the Truro Highlands. I picked a sunny spot on deck and dozed.

The squall sneaked up silently. The first sound I remember was not the wind but the worried murmur of voices in the cockpit. I felt the heel of the boat suddenly increase. When I went back to the cockpit, Dick was already there.

"What do you think?" he asked.

"I'd like the genoa off, okay?"

A huge, powerful sail, hard to manage in a blow.

"Ben and I will go forward and do it."

The wind came up very quickly to about twenty-five knots. The Wellfleet shore disappeared behind us in the scud. Visibility forward closed down to about a quarter mile. Ahead lay twenty miles of unbuoyed, although unobstructed, water before we would reach the canal entrance. It would lie on a lee shore – dangerous. An interesting variety of short, steep seas was making up astern.

148

I rounded the *Argo* up into the wind. The size of the boat now came into play. I could not see Ben and Dick out on the bowsprit; a vast, cluttered distance lay between us. Sandy took a position amidships from which to relay messages, but his shouts were inaudible against the rush of wind and the slap of luffing sails.

The bow plunged under oncoming seas and the men on the bowsprit were at risk. They wore no safety harnesses, which were not in general use then. I throttled back to ease the motion of the boat, and the temporary repair on the throttle linkage chose that moment to let go. We continued to power ahead, too fast. Later I heard that the bowsprit went deep under twice. But the genny was finally secured, and with Sandy's help the mainsail was then wrestled to the boom and safely furled.

Under motor and mizzen we ran before the storm. *Argo's* heavily built, slab-sided hull produced a markedly erratic motion. The extra speed imparted by the engine added to the problem, but I did not want to cut it and rely on the tiny mizzen and the windage of bare poles to get us home before dark. Also I half-suspected it might not start again when required in the canal. I certainly didn't feel I could leave it racing in neutral with the throttle set too high for the next few hours. I'd heard horror stories from skippers in the Caribbean charter business about runaway diesel engines that had overheated – and couldn't be shut down.

If there was one direction this vessel seemed to want to go, it was down. Something in the way she fought the wheel and yawed headstrong, headlong before the following seas gave me a sinking feeling. Whether this was sober judgment or mere upwelling of my anxiety, I do not know. I wonder where *Argo* is now, and how she has weathered her subsequent storms.

The wind had come up to thirty-something knots. I was busy spinning spokes when I felt the gaze of the pretty but pale-faced Dede fixed on me. She was standing braced in the companionway, her expression anxiously posing the unasked question: Are we going to survive? I peered into the blank fog with what confidence I could muster. It seemed to satisfy her. With feigned nonchalance I reached up with one hand and touched the mizzen over my head. The sail was hard as a board from the gale's pressure. I jerked my hand away as if my fingers had touched a hot frying pan.

Below, Ben moved the engine cover and crawled into a narrow space in an attempt to fix the throttle linkage. After half an hour he came up looking slightly seasick. Next day in calm water he was able to take care of the repair in ten minutes.

After two hours on a roughly-averaged compass course we were drawing close to the canal entrance between Sandwich and Sagamore. We peered into the white wooly mist and listened for the sound of breakers on the shore – a rocky one at Sagamore, sandy at Sandwich. After twenty minutes of strain we saw what appeared to be a webbed apparition poking above the fog bank in midair. It soon turned into the ghostly gray steel superstructure that carries the Sagamore Bridge across the canal, a mile inland from shore. A moment later the canal entrance-buoy popped out of the low-lying fog, one hundred yards dead ahead. A great relief, a lucky hit.

This practically ended our cruise. We lay at Onset for the next two days waiting for the weather to abate. It did not. Our charter was for a long four-day weekend, so I called the owner. He gave his okay to leave *Argo* tied up at the Onset boatyard, saying he had plans to cruise in that area later in the season.

The next summer I chartered a fifty-four-foot Alden

schooner, a strong horse of a boat, traditional green hull and gaff rig. We cruised Buzzards Bay and Nantucket Sound, enjoying the vessel and the weather. Within a couple of days the boat's size no longer seemed to matter.

But it's wiser not to leap into fifty-footers without first sailing the intermediate sizes, which are readily available from charter companies. Later in the evening on which *Argo* limped wearily into Onset at the far end of the canal, a boyhood friend of mine – a lieutenant commander in the naval reserve – was in command of a sizable patrol boat on training exercises off Marblehead. He had the misfortune to have his vessel go on the rocks and sink. No lives were lost, but his commission was, after a court martial. His expertise was overmatched by the size of the vessel under his command, in that kind of weather off a rocky coast. The same thing could have happened to anyone caught out on such a miserable night. Without the experience to handle his vessel in tough conditions, or in a vessel not prepared to meet the conditions, a sailor is risking his life, his crew's and those of his possible rescuers.

Since the cruise of the *Argo* I have made a special effort not to let that combination of circumstances occur when I go sailing. I hope you will feel encouraged to do likewise.

·23·

Companionship and Sailing
•

Sailing is not necessarily companionable, at least not in the usual sense of conversational chitchat. One of the chief pleasures of an afternoon's sail is its quietness. The lapping waves, a creaking block, sails luffing during a tack – these are the sounds of a happy boat. Small talk comes best when you are back on land, drinking beer, comparing notes at a party or bar.

The sounds of sailing also tell a story of the boat's speed, orientation to wind and wave, and general well-being. That is one reason to listen attentively. But only one. Pure pleasure in the absence of life's usual clatter is the other.

You will notice proof of this if, having powered out the channel in an auxiliary with several friends, you cut the engine and set sail. The ensuing silence brings expressions of relief from everyone. Sail on a while. Watch your friends each find a quiet spot on deck. One will stand at the bow rail and gaze at the ocean. Another will take the windward rail; one may perhaps prefer the leeward. Even those remaining in the cockpit are generally laconic as they fold into the sensation of motion under sail.

Occasionally you go sailing with someone who cannot stop talking or one whose company stimulates lots of conversation. You both return to shore frustrated, having missed something important. You are perhaps not the best-matched sailing companions.

Yet sailing provides much companionship. You share the feeling of being at one with the forces of nature. The soft embrace of water hugging a good hull, the thoroughbred action of the hull itself, is transmitted and received from person to person. Oral comments may be few but as the vessel heels to the wind, you are all borne not just on the same boat but on a common tide of feeling. Sometimes – as the boat leans, breeze freshens, waves slap – this swells until it seems the emotion alone could transport you. There are whoops and shouts of pleasure, smiles to pass along.

This is the best companionship of sail, the community of a lively vessel and its crew, waterborne.

Finish Line

•

Last autumn a man wanting to learn to sail called me. He had bought a daysailer and moored it in East Bay up toward the Centerville River. Would I come down and teach him, although the season had grown late?

September Sundays were warm last fall. After the morning Beetle races I took the Whaler out the cut and turned east, running down a mile or so of the Wianno shore past some houses grand and old, past Dowses Beach into the East Bay cut. On the beach at the landing I espied a slim, wiry, intense, and slightly nervous man in his early fifties. His companion was younger, mustachioed, relaxed.

On the daysailer it became apparent that the older man had read the sailing instruction books and become overcautious. In contrast, his son-in-law was as calm, understanding and open – and laid back about sailing – as ever a first-time sailor could be. He took the tiller first.

The breeze had come up, so we sailed in the bay and up the river. Easy going for son-in-law, father's worries evaporating. Now father on the tiller. A few bloops and then steady progress beating up the river, running back down, reaching across the bay. Finally they brought the boat in, moored, and furled without much help from me.

I did not get a call for the next two weeks. I thought my student had decided to sail on his own. But then came another call. This time father was alone and once again worried.

But the wind was light, the sailing easy. Soon it became clear that he could handle the boat alone quite well. I settled in as a passenger. He did it all, mooring, furling, putting the boat to bed.

In the remaining few weeks of decent weather I saw him weekends, puttering and fixing on his boat in the bay, occasionally sailing, looking unhurried and relaxed. His was the last sailboat in East Bay to be taken out for the winter. I think he has found his relaxation from onshore pressures. This spring I expect his boat to appear early on its mooring.

Earlier in the summer my son Mark came down with a friend for a couple of days on the Cape. We piled in the Whaler to go out to meet Steve, coming in from a junior series race in number 7. It was blowing eighteen knots or so. Steve had won a race – the first one ever for any of us in *Tirza*. At the mooring, Mark and his friend jumped on, the racing crew debarked. Steve stayed and we all headed back down the channel for a sail. Mark had the tiller now after years away from it, the wind up to twenty, the boat on her ear, everybody all grins, even Mark's friend – on her first sail – happily awash on the leeward cockpit seat and refusing to move to the high, dry side. A glorious sail! And to watch your kids enjoying it so!

One moonlit night after dinner, I slip down to the boat for a night sail. On West Bay a silver path of moonbeam points out the cut. It is August, and already a coolness permeates the light night breeze.

Not many more opportunities will come along this season. I raise only the main and follow the silvery path southwestward out the cut. All is silence but for the *wish* of lapping wavelets against the hull; all darkness but for glints of liquid moonbeam dancing on rippled water, shadowed white of sail, and stars spilled like diamonds tumbling across a black velvet vault.

I sit quietly as the boat floats through space. We reach Bell One, waking my reverie. The younger kids need putting to bed, someone in the house to secure them against the night. Besides it is getting chilly out here, and lonely too.

I sail back to the mooring and put the boat to bed. From the Whaler on the way to the dock I look back at her, so beautiful in repose.

Good night, boat. You have given much. Rest safely. We shall sail again in the morning.

Wianno Senior

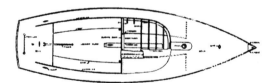

General Specifications

Dimensions – Length overall 25 ft., Length water line 17 ft., 6 in., Beam 8 ft.
Draft 2 ft., 6 in. without centerboard

Keel, Deadwoods and Stem – Native white oak.

Frames – Native white oak, steamed and bent to fit. $1\frac{1}{2}$" square, spaced
9 in. on centers, dovetailed and wedged to keel. Floor timbers native white oak.

Planking – Best quality $\frac{13}{16}$" air dried Honduras Mahogany, fastened with
Everdur bronze screws.

Rudder – Oak. Brass pipe sleeve and stock. Oak tiller with brass straps.

Acknowledgements

Much of the sailing and racing described in this book occurred with the aid and in the company of my older daughter, Deborah Ulian. Her calm concentration and athletic agility did not fail even when we were far behind the fleet and her two younger brothers had begun to gaze vacantly at the empty horizon. As the oldest she alone crewed for me on the longer delivery trips and informal races to regatta sites – among the pleasantest sails I've ever had. Thanks to Mark Ulian, beneath whose muscular foredeck work lay sailing skills one mightn't expect in a championship hockey player, and whose unflagging good humor made for a happy boat. And to Steve Ulian, about whom more below. These three made up the racing crew I sailed with for many years. They tried to impart patience to their father while he attempted to maintain credibility during a long losing streak. Pollena Ulian Forsman was too young at four to join in the racing but always great fun to have around.

A doff of the Ultimate Sailing Hat® to Steve, who went on after college to mount a credible Star-class Olympic campaign in 1988, and win a World Championship in 1992 in J/22s with crew Brad Dellenbaugh and Tommy Tompkins. During a seven-year career with North Sails he also won the Etchells North Americans three times (as tactician for Judd Smith once, and Dave Curtis twice) and had back-to-back 2nds in the J/24 Worlds (on the foredeck for Kevin Mahaney in Australia with tactician Curtis, John Alofsin and Tompkins, and calling tactics for Curtis in Canada). His comments helped sharpen the chapter on sails and others. The remaining fuzziness is mine.

Many thanks to Bud Lifton, loyal brother and faithful skipper of an Ensign 22 on Lake Michigan. His generosity and good counsel have helped my writing and living more than I can say. To Teddy Crosby at Crosby Yacht for his Cape Cod wit and inimitable boat-building skills – you can tell a boat he's worked on from twenty yards away. To Dick Whitman of 'Marstons Mills Marine,' whose ingenious repairs have constantly upgraded *Tirza's* seaworthiness and comfort. To the Wianno Senior Class Association and the Wianno Yacht Club for providing an enjoyable atmosphere in which to sail with keen competitors who love the sport. Like the Cotuit Mosquito Yacht Club, the WYC runs a top-flight sailing school for kids, available to the public. And thanks to the many Senior skippers who overlooked a very rusty racing sailor's gaffs and pitched in to help his learning curve trend upward in a complex, somewhat mysterious racing boat and hot fleet.

Thanks to Sally Davis, the children's mother. She rarely raced but sailed always with good sportsmanship after unselfishly encouraging *Tirza's* purchase.

Thanks to Van Nostrand Reinhold, N.Y., which first published *A Sailor's Notebook* [in an earlier version entitled *Sailing: An Informal Primer*] and to the Dolphin/Book-of-the-Month Club, which selected it as a featured book. Unfortunately the publisher put its trade book list up for sale a month later. The business remained in limbo, unsold for two years, scuttling marketing efforts for the book and a planned paperback edition. Many thanks to the e-publishers for beckoning the long-wandering *Sailor's Notebook* home from the briny, remote corners of the literary world and refitting her as a ship of the online.

May they all sail happily to the Finish Line.

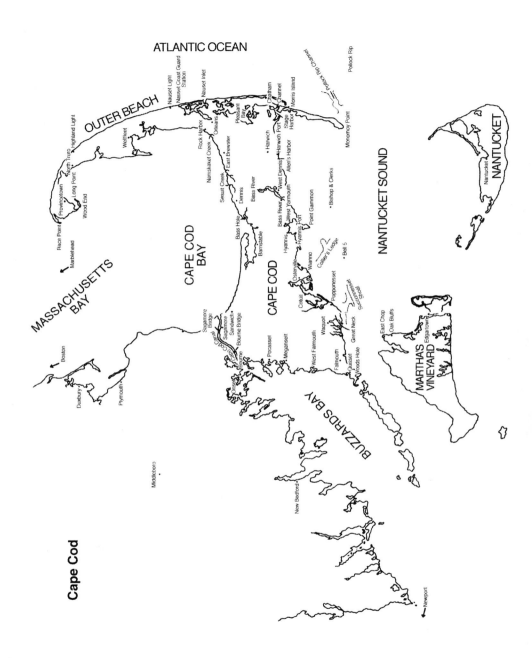

Cape Cod

ATLANTIC OCEAN

OUTER BEACH

MASSACHUSETTS BAY

CAPE COD BAY

CAPE COD

NANTUCKET SOUND

NANTUCKET

BUZZARDS BAY

MARTHA'S VINEYARD

Nauset Light
Nauset Coast Guard Station
Nauset Inlet
Pollock Rip
Pollock Rip Channel
Chatham
Chatham Channel
Morris Island
Stage Harbor
Monomoy Point
Pleasant Bay
Harwich Port
Harwich
West Dennis
Allen's Harbor
Bishop & Clerks
Point Gammon
Bell 5
Collier's Ledge
Wianno
Osterville
Poppanesset
Succonesset Shoal
Bass River
West Yarmouth
Hyannis Port
Hyannis
Cotuit
Rock Harbor
Orleans
Namskaket Creek
East Brewster
Sesuit Creek
Dennis
Bass River
Barnstable
Bass Hole
Wellfleet
North Truro
Highland Light
Long Point
Provincetown
Wood End
Race Point
Marblehead
Boston
Duxbury
Plymouth
Middleboro
New Bedford
Newport
Sagamore Bridge
Sagamore
Sandwich
Bourne Bridge
Cape Cod Canal
Canal
Bourne
Pocasset
Megansett
West Falmouth
Falmouth
Cataumet
Woods Hole
Waquoit
Great Neck
East Chop
Oak Bluffs
Edgartown

Nantucket